CAPE COD VOYAGE

*A Journey Through Cape Cod's
History and Lore*

CAPE COD VOYAGE

A Journey Through Cape Cod's History and Lore

Jim Coogan
Jack Sheedy

Harvest Home Books
East Dennis, Massachusetts

In cooperation with
The Barnstable Patriot
Hyannis, Massachusetts

And with special thanks to
Cape Cod Guide Magazine
Yarmouthport, Massachusetts

CAPE COD VOYAGE

First Printing – November 2001

Published by
Harvest Home Books, P.O. Box 1181
East Dennis, Massachusetts 02641

In cooperation with
The Barnstable Patriot, P.O. Box 1208
Hyannis, Massachusetts 02601

And with the permission of
Cape Cod Guide Magazine

ISBN 0-9672596-2-2

Cover design and text layout by Kristen vonHentschel

Printed in the United States of America

Additional copies of *Cape Cod Voyage*, or
the authors' previous book *Cape Cod Companion*,
may be obtained by contacting Harvest Home Books
or *The Barnstable Patriot* at the addresses above.

TABLE OF CONTENTS

TABLE OF CONTENTS Cont...

TABLE OF CONTENTS Cont...

TABLE OF CONTENTS Cont...

INTRODUCTION

It was former Speaker of the House of Representatives Thomas "Tip" O'Neill who said, "all politics is local." O'Neill, who spent a good bit of his later life at his summer home in Harwichport, would have also agreed that all history is local. For it is the bits and pieces of history made in small towns that fills out the texture of the wider nation. One can't begin to understand the whole without examining some of these little pieces that, by themselves, have little meaning unless connected by historians to a theme, a person, or a location.

The material in this book comes from some of the many pieces of historical flotsam and jetsam that I have collected over the years in researching material for my Cape Cod lecture series. I kept the information on index cards with the idea that someday they might evolve into feature stories about the Cape. Most of the facts and snippets, however, are probably too small to be articles in their own right. But these fragments from dusty archives and old newspapers are certainly more than just trivia. Like the pieces of a jigsaw puzzle, they need to be saved, noted, and remembered to give us a fuller picture of Cape Cod history.

Some of the stories in *Cape Cod Voyage* are admittedly whimsical and many are humorous. A few tend to be more serious, but all should be of interest to lovers of Cape Cod. I've always felt that historical trivia books, while entertaining, seemed incomplete because they do not amplify or explain where information came from. As a result, while piquing interest, they don't make it easy for casual readers to move further into the subject. A glance at the sources for the stories that are featured in this book should give anyone who is serious about going beyond the topic a firm place to start.

Thus, in a spirit of fun and fascination, I've worked with my co-author Jack Sheedy to put together a book about Cape Cod that is both serious and entertaining. Our collection of essays is designed to showcase some of the lesser known and interesting sides of Cape Cod history. It is an effort to bring to light some new aspects and information about this most fascinating peninsula. And, unlike a simple trivia book, *Cape Cod Voyage* will supply more than just a one-word answer.

I hope you enjoy our efforts.

Jim Coogan
October, 2001
Dennis, Massachusetts

FOREWORD

Each year, in August, I give a little talk on the subject of Cape Cod history before a group of children at the Dennis Public Library. We explore a spectrum of topics from lighthouses to sea captains to cranberries. I'd say the average age of the children is about eight or nine years old.

I realized a few years back when I first started doing these talks that nearly 400 years of history is sometimes a difficult notion for children to understand. So I put together a time line in the form of a long roll of paper, measuring some 14 feet in length, to represent the many years from today back to 1620 and the arrival of the Pilgrims. Along the way are key historical events to give them a sense of the march of time – man landing on the moon, the sinking of the *Titanic*, the time of Lincoln, Washington, etc. A mere four inches at the very top of the paper represent the short span of the children's young lives thus far, while the remaining 13 feet and eight inches depicts their "pre-history" back to the age of the *Mayflower*. This provides them with a graphic representation of the breadth of our collective Cape Cod history and gives them an idea of how long ago a particular historical event occurred.

As adults, we sometimes forget to appreciate the span of the history that came before us, even here within our own small corner of the world. My own family history in New England, for example, goes back to the mid-nineteenth century. Though this may seem like a good chunk of time, consider that when my first ancestors arrived here from the Emerald Isles there already existed over 200 years of New England and Cape Cod history preceding them. Even at that time, in the 1840s, the Pilgrims, the colonists, and those of the Revolutionary era were already considered legends.

A good amount of our country's early history is entwined with the history of this outermost peninsula we know as Cape Cod. Earliest European explorers such as Bartholomew Gosnold and

Samuel de Champlain arrived here before the Pilgrims ... Gosnold in 1602 at which time he named this place for the multitude of codfish. When the Pilgrims did step foot in the New World, they first did so upon the sandy soil of Provincetown about one month before the rocky coast of Plymouth. In fact, a number of the Cape's earliest settlers, during the 1630s and 1640s, were Pilgrims or the offspring of Pilgrims.

So, it is with a deep appreciation for the past that my co-author Jim Coogan and I embark on this latest voyage upon the ocean of Cape Cod history. Our earlier effort, entitled *Cape Cod Companion*, was published in 1999 with over 50 tales written throughout the 1990s as appearing in the *Barnstable Patriot's* annual history magazine *Summerscape*.

This latest collection of tales began life in a different way. A couple of years ago, Jim approached me with a collection of stories he compiled over many years of research with the thought that a number of these stories could be published in our next collaborative effort. I then added tales I had written for a number of *Barnstable Patriot* publications such as *Summerscape* and their fleet of town books, as well as some articles I had done for *Cape Cod Guide Magazine* and some stories written specifically for this collection. The result, after many months of editing, proofreading, and refining is the compilation you hold in your hands – over 100 tales from four centuries.

We hope you enjoy our latest journey through Cape Cod's history and lore. It is a voyage that began long, long ago ... and which is continuing onward even today.

Jack Sheedy, Editor
October, 2001
Dennis, Massachusetts

Chapter
1

Places Plain & Peculiar

Over the years there have been more than a few disappointed tourists who have driven to Bourne in search of the monument at Monument Beach. In fact, there is no monument at or near this expanse of sand just north of Toby's Island.

As with many place names on Cape Cod, Monument Beach comes most likely from the Algonquian Indian word "manamet," which translates roughly to mean "the trail of the burden carriers." While this may confuse modern day tourists, it is actually an appropriate name for the area because it was near here that Native people, and later, early European settlers, portaged cargo across the small river that eventually became the western entrance to the Cape Cod Canal.

Indian names, traditional designations of areas named after long forgotten geographical features, and nicknames of places whose origins have faded with time can often confuse visitors who are trying to navigate their way around the peninsula.

Similarly, Cape Codders themselves are often guilty of letting their pride go before geographical accuracy, which can also further the difficulty of locating a particular place. If, for example, a person were to inquire where the highest hill on Cape Cod is located, there would be a variety of responses from local residents. In Dennis, well-meaning townspeople would point convincingly toward Scargo Hill. In Brewster they would say it was Cannon Hill. If the question were asked in Barnstable, the answer would be given with just as much conviction that it was Shootflying Hill above Lake Wequaquet! In fact, the highest natural point on Cape Cod is in the village of Pocasset, in the town of Bourne, at Pine Hill on the Buzzards Bay Moraine. That lofty point has been measured by the U.S. Geological Survey team at 306 feet above sea level.

In our introductory chapter we will take a look at some of the places and place names that make Cape Cod unique. Our journey will take us from Puckertown to Punkhorn to Physic Point, and to many places in between.

A Sense of Where We Were

It wasn't that long ago that you could get on a Cape Cod road and pretty much know where you were going to end up, and what you were going to see along the way. Harwich Road was just that - the way to Harwich.

The same is true for streets like Bridge Street, Depot Street, or High School Road. But many of the physical and cultural reference points that used to tell us where we were are gradually being lost in the onrush of new subdivisions, long-established and familiar store closings, and the substitution of route numbers for long-held road names. (Harwich Road is now generally better known by Brewster residents as Route 124.) There is something of the charm and character of a place that is lost when generic names replace a collection of former touchstones that made a community unique.

Fishermen often described locations in some of the most colorful and memorable language. For example, "Tempest Knob" was located near Buzzards Bay. In Pleasant Bay and Nauset Marsh on the lower Cape they located their positions referring to place names like "Flat Fish Hold," "Fox Bar," "Money Head," "Hole in the Wall," and "Venie's Slough." The latter was probably named for former Wellfleet Shellfish Warden Venie Pierce. Even more

colorful were places like "Lucy's Crotch" and other location names
that the editors deemed too risqué to appear in this book. In earlier
days, you certainly knew where you were!

Near Scorton Hill in East Sandwich there is an area that used to
be called "Honey Bottom." Pocasset has an area that was once
referred to as "Putt's Hollow." In West Brewster there is a long
gentle bend in the state road east of the Cape Cod Museum of
Natural History. Few people refer to it as "Betty's Curve" any
more. The name, no doubt, refers to the memory of a shapely
female member of the Paine, Winslow, or Newcomb family.

Sections of towns once had unusual names that have mostly
fallen away from modern maps. West Barnstable, for example, was
once called "Finntown" because of the large numbers of inhabitants who had immigrated from Finland. Woods Hole in Falmouth
was once "Holmes Hole" and Provincetown was "Herrington."

A section of Hyannis was referred to as "Happy Hollow." Few
present day residents of Orleans would know that "Sand City"
was the name given to the large number of summer cottages that
were on the Atlantic at Nauset Beach in the first years of this
century. Still fewer Dennis residents would know that "Halltown"
was a section of north Dennis and that "Sandy Bottom" was the
area of South Dennis near the present Water District building.
There was a part of Truro near Great Hollow Road that went by the
name "Whitmanville." Puckertown was a section of Wellfleet and
it is not known as to whether the inhabitants there were especially
good kissers.

Interestingly, Wellfleet was originally named "Poole," probably
after an English seaport in Dorset on the east coast of Britain. The
end of the name, "fleet," may well have had its origin in the Saxon
word "floet," or "flete," which means a place where the tide comes
in. In England, Wellfleet was where a wall was put up on the north
side of Blackwater Bay to hold back the sea.

"Odd Twists of Time and Tongue"

It is believed that the village names of Hyannis and Wianno were
derived from the Cummaquid Indian Sachem Iyanough, and the

many misinterpretations, misspellings and mispronunciations of his name over the centuries.

In his book *Cape Cod Ahoy!*, Arthur Wilson Tarbell alliteratively refers to these misinterpretations, misspellings and mispronunciations as "odd twists of time and tongue." This connection between Iyanough, Hyannis, and Wianno may very well be true.

Yet, it seems that the origins of the village names Hyannis and Wianno may equally have come from the many misinterpretations, misspellings and mispronunciations of another Barnstable Indian sachem by the name of Yanno. It further seems that Yanno was the son and heir of the famous Iyanough.

According to the 1939 book *Barnstable: Three Centuries of a Cape Cod Town* by Barnstable historian Donald G. Trayser, Sachem Yanno began transferring ownership of the lands comprising Hyannis, Hyannisport and Centerville over to white settlers in the year 1664. At that time the newly acquired landscape was known as Yanno or Yanno's Land and in the 1670s the harbor was known as Yanno Harbour. Around 1690 the name Yannows appears on deeds, and in the early 1700s the spelling Higheinnes appears on at least one map. Throughout the eighteenth century the village of

Statue of Cummaquid Indian Iyanough at Hyannis village green. (A. Sheedy photo)

Hyannis answered to the following names: Jannos, Iyannos, Hyannos, Hyanos, Hyanus, Yannis, Hianna, Hiannas, Highannus, Hiannis, and Hyanis. By 1800, the accepted spelling of the village became "Hyannis."

Necks

Cape Cod is a veritable collection of body parts. There are shoulders, an elbow, several heads, a forearm - even an exposed backside! But perhaps more than anything else there are necks - plenty of them.

One wag even said that Cape Codders could legitimately be called "neckers" given the quantity and distribution of such geographical locations. Without falling back on "little neck," here is a list of Cape Cod necks:

There's Barley Neck and Smith Neck (Orleans), Wings Neck, Barlows Neck, Bennett Neck, Little Monument Neck, and Scraggy Neck (Bourne), Chequessett Neck, Coles's Neck, and Indian Neck (Wellfleet), Crocker's Neck, Oak Neck, Baxter Neck, Dead Neck, Carseley Neck, Nyes' Neck, and Huckins Neck (Barnstable).

But wait, there's more. There's Plowed Neck, Scorton Neck, Sandy Neck, Canaumet Neck, and Town Neck (Sandwich), Meadow Neck, Bar Neck, and Nyes' Neck (Falmouth), Great Neck and Bryant's Neck (Mashpee), Simpkins Neck, Crocker's Neck, Quivet Neck, and Sesuit Neck (Dennis), Taylor's Neck, Nickerson's Neck, Tom's Neck (Chatham), Eagle's Neck (Truro), and Bell's Neck and Grey Neck in Harwich. Undoubtedly, there are a few more that have escaped this list.

All of this proves that in this neck of the woods you can always find one.

A Place Called Punkhorn

A large section of the southwest portion of the town of Brewster, once home to generations of hardscrabble farmers, was set aside as a conservation area called "Punkhorn Parklands."

The so-called "Punkhorn" region has always been a place of

quiet natural beauty and because of the foresight of the towns-people, some 835 acres have been set aside for public use. The Indian translation of the name Punkhorn roughly means "place of spongy wood." With a number of abandoned cranberry bogs and swamp areas, the description is still accurate.

Some local people tell of a tribe of Punkhorn Indians that once inhabited the area, but that story seems to parallel the tales of the so-called fictional "Figawi" tribe of Barnstable. Archaeological studies of the Punkhorn area do indicate a pre-Columbian pres-ence of Native people who lived along the shores of the two mill ponds that are within the parklands boundaries. Several trails lead along the high eastern bluffs above the ponds and it is easy to imagine the first human inhabitants of the area encamped here. Interestingly, in Mashpee, the Land of the Wampanoag, there is a place called Punkhorn Point, located off Great Neck Road on the way to South Cape Beach.

Writer Geneva Eldredge has left us with a formula for what she calls "Punkhorn Stew," an old family recipe that was once com-mon on Cape Cod. In October her father would store salted pieces of pork from the fall hog slaughtering in a stone crock in the cellar. Here the meat would sit for most of the winter and then when it came time to make the stew, her mother would cut up some of the pork and simmer it in water for a couple of hours in a covered pot on the wood stove.

Vegetables, including slices of white turnip (Eastham turnips, no doubt), parsnips, carrots, small onions, and large-size potatoes cut lengthwise, would be peeled and added to the pork. Additional seasonings and water were added to the mix, which was then cooked for another hour. The final stage was the removal of the lid on the pot and the insertion of thick chunks of brown bread crust over the top of the stew. The pot would then be recovered and left to steam on low heat for a final fifteen minutes.

Upper and Lower Cape Cod

Ask any self-respecting resident of Orleans, Eastham, Wellfleet, Truro, and Provincetown, and they will say they live on the "outer" Cape. It makes sense when you look at the map and the shape of the peninsula. But, does that mean that there is a corresponding "inner" Cape?

The most common and misunderstood terms of description are "upper" and "lower" Cape. It has been suggested that the terms actually described two distinct social class areas of Cape Cod, based on what kinds of cars are parked in the garages of certain villages – for example, Infinities and Range Rovers in Osterville; Chevrolets and Fords in Wellfleet. It has also been said that there are more Wall Street Journals delivered in the village of Cotuit, while the Boston Herald is the print medium of choice for Eastham.

The real answer can be found by looking to the days of sail. The prevailing westerly winds caused vessels to sail downwind while going northeasterly and upwind while sailing southwesterly. So a vessel headed north from Barnstable across the bay toward Provincetown would be sailing "down" rather than "up" even though an examination of a map shows the opposite to be true. Thus it is that people from Providence or Boston say that they are going "down" the Cape for the weekend. It all makes perfect sense.

"Friends" Village

Early settlement of the town of Yarmouth occurred along the northern and eastern territories, the northern part today referred to as Yarmouthport and the eastern part now known as the town of Dennis (which broke away from its parent town in 1793).

The southern territory, especially the area southwest of Bass River, was left for a time to the Native Indians who were, decade by decade, being forced into smaller and smaller living spaces. The current village of South Yarmouth was initially referred to as Indian Town for the Natives who harvested shellfish along the banks of the river.

Yet, as the Bass River Indian population dwindled the area became attractive to another group of castaways, namely the Quakers, or "Friends," who were being forced out of other towns such as Sandwich where they were not wanted by the much larger Congregational population. South Yarmouth became a haven for this persecuted group as they escaped the "wrath of the righteous."

Quakers first appeared in the area of South Yarmouth around the mid-eighteenth century at a time when smallpox was in the process of wiping out the Indians. Notable South Yarmouth Quaker David Kelley arrived in 1790 and many others followed. "First Day," or Sunday services commenced at a meeting house built around the turn of the nineteenth century at Follins Pond in neighboring Dennis. Services moved to South Yarmouth where a meetinghouse was built around 1809. That building, and its adjoining cemetery of simple, white headstones remains to this day at the corner of North Main Street and Kelley Road. The meetinghouse is beautiful in its simplicity, without decoration and with modest natural pews within. Of interest is a wall that runs down the middle of the building that is said to have segregated the men and women during service.

The Quakers of South Yarmouth were industrious to say the least. In the late eighteenth century they operated the Farris Windmill, relocated to South Yarmouth from the north side of

Quaker meetinghouse and cemetery at South Yarmouth, dating to the early nineteenth century. (J. Sheedy photo)

town. During much of the nineteenth century they built many saltworks along Bass River and an elaborate ropewalk next to the meetinghouse. As saltworks shut down toward the end of the nineteenth century a wire works was established. Over time, Methodists and Baptists also found South Yarmouth to their liking. Meanwhile, the Friends population of South Yarmouth diminished as intermarriages between Quakers and non-Quakers took members out of the ranks both physically and religiously.

Physic Point

In days of old, people would occasionally mention that they were going to take a "physic" to settle their troubled stomach. In fact, Cape Cod once had whole villages that suffered from such ailments as gastric catarrh, dyspepsia, and all sorts of forms of "bilious diseases."

One could purchase Doctor William's Vegetable Bitters - "The People's Remedy," or perhaps Perry Davis' Vegetable Pain Killer, which cured cholera, dysentery and "other kindred complaints." In Wellfleet, Doctor Warren Anson Kenrick prescribed a variety of "physics" to the point that the section of town where he lived became known as "Physic Point." Another "Physic Point" could be found in Hyannis where Mrs. Liza Baker dispensed generous doses of castor oil laced with laxative to purge the bad digestive humors of children who lived near Ocean Street.

Billingsgate Island - A Victim of the Tides

There was once an old-timer who was fond of saying, "Time and the tides wait for no man." Nowhere is this more true than here on Cape Cod, especially in regard to the unceasing march of the tides.

Cape Cod is a peninsula in a constant state of flux. Over the millennia its shape has been altered repeatedly by the combination of wave and wind with formulae forever random. Five to ten thousand years ago, when the Indians began to appear on Cape Cod, it is believed that much of Cape Cod Bay was dry. The hemisphere was still recovering from the last ice age during which much of the earth's water was stored in mammoth ice sheets.

A thousand years ago, around the time when Basque fishermen and Norse explorers were frequenting these shores, the sea level was still quite a bit lower than it is today. Around Cape Cod, landmasses existed that are now long gone.

Nearly four centuries ago the *Mayflower* Pilgrims arrived first at Cape Cod before journeying onward to start their lives at Plimoth. While on the outer arm of the peninsula, in December 1620, they ventured along the coastline to explore the lands known today as Provincetown, Truro, Wellfleet, and Eastham. On the bay side of Wellfleet they happened upon a long tapering outer beach with an island off to the south. The Pilgrims noticed that along the beach were a number of Native Indians, known as the Pononakanit, carving blubber off some "blackfish," most likely pilot whales. These leviathans had either beached themselves in the shallows or else were captured by the Pononakanit out in the bay. Some reports state that it was the Pilgrims themselves who named the island and the nearby land Billingsgate because the multitude of fish reminded them of a London fish market that went by that same name.

Settlement of the area began rather early, in 1644, by Pilgrims who ventured southeast from Plimoth Colony. First known as Nauset, and later as the town of Eastham, the area of Billingsgate resided in the northern territory of the new settlement. Legend has it that when the land was purchased from the Indians the settlers asked, "Who owns the land to the north?" The Indians answered, "No one owns the land." So the settlers quickly announced, "Then, we own it." That land today comprises the towns of Wellfleet, Truro, and Provincetown.

It is believed that settlement of Billingsgate began on her islands, mainly Great Island, Griffins (also referred to as Griffith's) Island, Lieutenants Island, and at Billingsgate Island. The smallest of the four, Billingsgate Island was about three-quarters of a mile to a mile long and perhaps a quarter to a half-mile wide at its most extreme point. It was triangular in shape and rested three miles out into the bay due west of Hatches Creek at the border of Eastham and Wellfleet.

Around 1722, the settlement of Billingsgate was considering a separation from its parent town of Eastham. It would take over 40 years before permission was granted, which occurred in May 1763. By that time, the area had become as famous for its rich oyster beds as for its whaling and fishing fleets. So, those who decided such things changed the name of the new town from Billingsgate to Wellfleet.

Meanwhile, the little island out at the entrance to Wellfleet Harbor maintained its Billingsgate name, keeping alive the memory of the fifteenth-century London fish market of the Pilgrims' former English homeland.

As early as the 1730s there was a tryworks on the island for harvesting whale oil. During the 1750s the island and nearby beaches became the scene of a battle over who had the rights to use the land as a whaling station. Native Indians from nearby Eastham had made use of the island for years, yet the Europeans could clearly see the importance of an island so close to the Cape Cod Bay whaling grounds. Over the following years, though, the Indian population diminished for a number of reasons, among them plagues, and by the beginning of the nineteenth century there is mention in the Wellfleet town records of only one remaining Indian woman. Ownership of the island, at least as it applied to Native inhabitants, was therefore resolved by attrition.

Over the course of the nineteenth century a small village community sprung up on the island consisting of over 30 houses, a store, a schoolhouse, the tryworks, a wharf, and five whaling vessels as well as a fishing fleet. In 1822, a brick lighthouse and adjoining keeper's dwelling were erected on the eastern shore of the island. This original lighthouse tower was about 40 feet above the waves and had eight lamps to cast its beam. According to historian Edward Rowe Snow in his book *The Lighthouses of New England,* the ocean began to threaten the island toward the middle part of the century. As the Civil War approached, likewise did the waters of Cape Cod Bay around Billingsgate Light. A new red brick lighthouse was constructed on higher ground in 1858, yet the waves of the bay continued their assault on the island.

Within 20 years much of the island was awash during extreme high tides. Homes were torn down and ferried across the water to the mainland. Families vacated the island for higher and drier ground. By the 1870s only eight houses containing eight hardy families remained. Yet the tides kept coming and in the 1880s bulkhead walls were built around the lighthouse to protect her from the waves. After one high tide in 1876 the lighthouse keeper was found adrift on his boat in Cape Cod Bay, dead.

In 1882, the new keeper of the light reported that five feet of water covered the island during high tide, except for a 30-foot circle around the lighthouse. By the beginning of the twentieth century even the hardiest of families vacated the disappearing island, leaving only the lighthouse keeper and the oyster bed watchmen to document the death throes of a once thriving community.

The year 1915 marked the end of Billingsgate Light. With the waters of Cape Cod Bay marching on the building, the keeper evacuated and the light was removed from the tower. A temporary light was installed at the eastern end of what remained to warn mariners of the shoal that Billingsgate had become. By 1922, even that light was discontinued. Remarkably, an over 50-acre island that once supported vegetation, wildlife, a lighthouse, and a busy fishing and whaling community had been wiped clear away by the relentless sea.

A Bostonian purchased the shrinking island, at that time no larger than five acres, and built a hunting lodge from the materials that comprised the abandoned buildings. Later, Billingsgate became a bird sanctuary. By 1935 the island was no more. In Josef Berger's 1937 book *Cape Cod Pilot* the author reports: "Wellfleet has recently lost an island. The ocean, like an indecisive sculptor, putters around with Cape Cod, chipping off here and slapping on there, to suit its mood of the moment; and the recent disappearance of the island of Billingsgate is one of its most striking changes in the design."

For well over a century the sea provided the residents of Billingsgate with their livelihood, and in the end the sea took it all away. A mighty fishing and whaling community was no match for the myriad of waves that one by one shaped and eventually devoured an entire island. As that old-timer with pipe in mouth once said, "Time and the tides ... they wait for no man."

Chapter
2

Mooners & Mooncussers

Regional speech patterns have pretty much gone by the boards with the homogenizing effect of television. We are now several generations removed from the traditional "Capespeak" dialect that is featured in the early twentieth century novels of Joseph C. Lincoln. When he wrote his books, he was aware that the particular way of speaking as expressed by his characters was already fading away.

The insulated atmosphere of Cape Cod, at least as it was up until the post World War II period, tended to keep in use some of the colloquialisms that had always been part of the culture. When we hear a person say "It was *some* cold last night," we can visualize some of the Cape Codders from generations past. Pronunciations of words like "summah," "wintah," and "buildin" can still serve to set the local clam diggers apart from the city folk.

There are still people who will say "Awleens" instead of the more wash-ashore pronunciation of "Oarleens" when referring to the town east of Brewster. And it's possible to find a few old timers who will put the emphasis on the "ham" in Eastham and

Wareham. But for the most part, words like "feetening," which
meant footprints, and "cruelize," which described cruelty toward
man or beast, can be found only in books, not in contemporary
conversation.

Still, something seems to be lost in the absence of descriptive
phrases and words such as "poslin around," which meant not
getting anywhere. Clam diggers used "dreeners" to hold their
shellfish and people lived in "housen" in old Cape Cod. To go
"up street" was to go downtown and having "leeway" and
"slewage" meant having plenty of room to move around. Just
about all of these figures of speech are now just memories. But
one can still hear a few of them. An old Cape Cod term that is
still occasionally uttered is "chowderhead," or "chow-da-head,"
which refers to a particularly dumb person. It is a timeless
reference, as applicable today when used by Cape Codders as it
was relevant a century ago.

Moons Over Stage Harbor

In October of 1606, Samuel de Champlain arrived in Chatham's
Stage Harbor. It was not the first visit to Cape Cod by the explorer
as he spent the preceding summer charting the New England
coastline while searching for a site to found a warmer version of
New France. Champlain anchored in Nauset Harbor that previous
year and was impressed with the landscape that he observed. He
made extensive and accurate drawings of the area with the full
intention of returning to establish a colony.

The second year saw his small band of adventurers navigating
around what he called "Cape Mallebare" in the area of present-day
Nauset Beach and entering an anchorage he called "Port Fortune."
This was the present Stage Harbor in Chatham. The location did not,
however, prove to be good fortune for Champlain. Relations with
the Native people turned sour after it appeared that they were
making themselves too familiar with the French supplies. A bloody
fight ensued wherein several of Champlain's men were killed.
Outnumbered, the French were forced to retreat to their ship.

Without a corresponding written account by the Indians, it is

A drawing, attributed to Champlain, depicting the Natives "turning the other cheek" at Stage Harbor, Chatham. (William Brewster Nickerson Room Collection - Cape Cod Community College)

probably wrong to simply accept the French account of where the guilt for the conflict rested, but the Native people showed their contempt for the retreating Europeans in a particularly rude manner. They repeatedly dug up the bodies of the dead Frenchmen and tore down the cross that was placed on the gravesite. In addition, as Champlain described their behavior in his journal, the Indians exhibited their contempt toward the French by "Turning their backs toward the barque (ship), they did cast sand with their two hands betwixt their buttocks in derision, howling like wolves."

The image is pretty clear. It would appear that Champlain and his crew were "mooned" by the Natives, the first recorded case of such an insult in the history of the Western Hemisphere.

America's First Dysfunctional Family

The history books paint a picture of the Pilgrims as "saints," incapable of doing any wrong. Clearly there were legendary souls among them. The names of Bradford, Brewster, Hopkins, Standish,

Winslow, and Alden seem to rise to the top of the list.

Yet, there was one family on the *Mayflower* that did not seem to fit in from the start. They were definitely not "Saints" and there is some question as to whether they were even "Pilgrims" in the strict sense of the word. William Bradford, in his journal entries, wrote: "They came from London, and I know not by what friends shuffled into their company."

Nobody seemed to know how they mingled into the Pilgrim flock, nor how they made their way onto the *Mayflower*, yet here they were amongst them as the vessel anchored in Cape Cod Bay. They were the Billingtons, Mr. and Mrs. John, and sons Francis and John, Jr. They were America's first dysfunctional family ... loose in the wilds of Plimoth Colony!

The drama began before the *Mayflower* even reached Plimoth. With the vessel anchored off Provincetown, young Francis celebrated the safe arrival by shooting off a musket and a fowling

The Mayflower II, *a replica of the original* Mayflower, *which young Francis Billington nearly blew up in Provincetown Harbor upon its arrival in 1620. (A. Sheedy photo)*

piece in the cabin, dangerously close to powder kegs. The *May-flower* was nearly blown up by the boy, and the Pilgrims along with her. Plimoth Colony was almost snuffed out then and there.

Fortunately, the *Mayflower* did not blow up and Francis' father lived to play a role in a rather important piece of parchment. John Billington's signature appears on the Mayflower Compact drawn up "at Cape Cod, the 11 of November," a document scripted to "combine ourselves together into a civil body politic." Yet Billington's uncivil behavior would begin to surface just four months later.

In March 1621, he became Plimoth's first public offender "for his contempt of Captain Myles Standish's lawful command with opprobrious speeches." Essentially, he swore at Standish. He also refused to take his turn at sentry duty. For his offense, he was sentenced to 24 hours of public punishment consisting of having his feet and head tied together. Billington was eventually pardoned because he was the Colony's first offender, although some reports state that he endured one hour of punishment before he was released.

Bradford wrote of Billington: "He and some of his had been often punished for miscarriages before, being one of the profanest families among them." He was described by author Gleason L. Archer, who wrote *With Axe and Musket at Plymouth*, as "profane and quarrelsome." Author Frederick A. Noble, in his book *The Pilgrims*, wrote: "He was a bad man at the start, and he was a bad man all through. He well deserved his fate."

Now it was son John's turn to cause some havoc. In July 1621, six-year old John Billington, Jr. became hopelessly lost in the forest south of Plimoth. After a fruitless one-week search of the surrounding woodlands the boy was given up for dead. Yet he was not dead. The mischievous child turned up 20 miles away at the Indian village of Manomet. Young Billington was then taken across the Cape to Nauset Sachem Aspinet where the Pilgrims later collected him.

By 1630, young John Billington, Jr. had died, cause uncertain. During that year his father would also be killed, hanged as Plimoth Colony's first convicted murderer. It is believed that the whole ordeal began with a quarrel between Billington and his victim, John Newcomen, possibly over the subject of hunting. Later, Billington hid in the woodlands and accosted Newcomen as he walked by. Newcomen tried to flee but was shot in the shoulder and left to bleed. Two witnesses saw Billington flee the scene.

Newcomen was taken from the woods and treated for his wound, but his condition worsened. A deposition was taken from the dying man naming Billington as his assailant. Bradford then sent Captain Standish and his men out to arrest the criminal, though he was not to be found. The next morning Billington sauntered home carrying game as if he was away hunting and knew nothing of the shooting. He was swiftly arrested and charged with attempted murder.

Despite days of prayer and the best efforts of the local doctor, Newcomen died, thus making Billington a murderer. At his trial, Billington defended himself claiming that the Plimoth Court did not have the authority in its patent to decide matters of life and death, and if they did decide for the death penalty then the Colony itself would be guilty of murder.

Though Bradford believed that the laws of England gave them the authority to act, some of the other men of Plimoth had doubts. They even considered sending Billington to England to stand trial. Instead, they consulted with Governor John Winthrop of neighboring Massachusetts Bay Colony who agreed with Bradford that Plimoth had the power to hand down the sentence of death. So, in September 1630, Pilgrim John Billington was hanged to death.

Six years after her husband's death, Mrs. Billington found herself in trouble with the law. It seems that in 1636 she was found guilty of slandering Deacon John Doane and was put in the stocks as punishment. She was also publicly whipped and was assessed a fine for her actions.

Today, reminders of John Billington and his family can be found in two notable places: upon copies of the Mayflower Compact where his signature appears as the 26th of the 41 signatories, and at Billington Sea, a large pond in Plymouth supposedly discovered by son Francis while climbing a tree.

A Man for One Season

The land that now comprises Yarmouth was a vast wilderness nearly three decades ago when a small group of settlers arrived around 1637 or 1638. This group, which was described by Governor John Winthrop as "being all poor men," was lead by a Reverend Stephen Bachiler who planned to tame this area far removed from Plimoth.

The facts concerning the "good" Reverend are varied, but it appears that from the start Bachiler did not have what it took to lead such an undertaking as the settlement of a village. In fact, Cape historian Amos Otis went so far as to write, "Mr. Bachiler was not such a man as a minister of the gospel should be." At the time when Bachiler made his ill-fated "pilgrimage" to Mattacheese, as these lands were called, he was in his mid-seventies ... an age when most men are settling into retirement. Yet Bachiler was anything but retiring. Winthrop writes of Bachiler and his trip to Mattacheese as "being about seventy-six years of age; yet he walked thither on foot at very hard season." It was a very hard season indeed, a most severe winter when he and his band arrived in this new land along the eastern portion of Mattacheese, "six miles beyond Sandwich" according to Winthrop.

Though the Native Indians helped Bachiler's group get through the harsh winter, the Englishmen decided in the end to pack up their belongings and move on. Yet Reverend Bachiler's exploits were far from over. He left for Newbury and later ended up in New Hampshire. Twice a widower, he took a third wife while in Portsmouth at age 81, a "lusty comely woman" according to Winthrop, yet the Reverend became interested in his neighbor's wife and was subsequently excommunicated for "unchastity."

In his late eighties, Bachiler decided he had had enough of the New World. He walked from Kittery to Boston and sailed back to England from whence he had come many years before. He then married again, although he neglected to divorce his previous wife, which caused all kinds of trouble. Near London, at about the age of one hundred, Bachiler finally passed away with his latest wife by his bedside.

The Legend of Hannah Screecham

The southern villages of Cotuit and Osterville share a tale centuries old and brimming with ghosts, pirates, buried treasures, and murder. It is the cobwebbed legend of Hannah Screecham, also known as Screecher, who lived alone on haunted Grand Island. The island, flanked by Cotuit Bay and West Bay, is today better known as Oyster Harbors.

At one time Hannah lived on the island with her sister, Sarah. Locals believed the two were demonic and left them alone to their satanic activities. Yet after an argument the two sisters parted company. Hannah remained at the island while Sarah, who was considered by the townsfolk to be a witch, removed herself to the forests of South Mashpee where she lived near what was appropriately called Witches Pond.

As for sister Hannah, the stories are many and varied. Some tell of her befriending pirates who frequented these shores, notably Captain Kidd, and helping them to bury their treasures in the dunes of Grand Island. Once, it is told, she directed one of Kidd's crewmen to a certain place on the island where he was instructed to dig a deep hole and bury the treasure of gold bars and coins. When he was finished, Hannah pushed him in the hole and buried him alive. It was said that she finished off many pirates in this fashion, and that her demonic wailing filled the air around the island, scaring away even the saltiest of seafarers. It was also said that whenever she attempted to dig up any of the gold for herself, the ghosts of those pirates whom she had earlier killed and buried would rise from their graves and prevent her from obtaining the treasures.

A contrary story states that one night the pirates discovered Hannah while they were burying their treasure so they murdered her and buried her along with their gold. Either way, for centuries it was believed that the ghost of Hannah Screecham haunted Grand Island, as witnessed by her screeching wail across the dunes at night, sending shivers through the sails of passing vessels.

Mooncussers

Shipwrecks along the Cape Cod coast meant lots of work for

local "wreckers" and salvagers. These were legitimate entrepreneurs who, like anchor draggers, would contract out their services to salvage whatever might be saved from vessels that had come ashore.

It seems, however, that some Cape Codders were perhaps a bit too eager for wrecks and these individuals hit on a scheme that would have a person on the shore swinging a simulated stern light on a moonless night. Ships at sea without the benefit of a moonlit horizon became confused as to their navigation and would be lured by the false light onto the shoreline where they were wrecked. The ship would then be plundered by the mooncussers who had no use for full moon nights when they could not do their dirty work. They cursed the light of the bright moon because it allowed ships to steer clear of disaster.

There is even some evidence to indicate that opposition to the building of lighthouses on Cape Cod came from families who had a vested interest in seeing that navigation would not be improved for passing ships. In Chatham there was a section of town up by the lighthouse on James' Bluff where a community of wreckers lived. Seaview Avenue in Chatham was once called "Wicked Hill" because there were stories of people who tied a lantern to a lame horse and then walked the animal back and forth along the beach to simulate a vessel at anchor. This had the effect of causing unsuspecting ships to be wrecked off Chatham Bars as they sought a safe anchorage.

The wrecking business in Chatham was apparently so prominent that in Rudyard Kipling's book *Captains Courageous*, there is a quote that says, "Ye scrabbletowners, Ye Chatham wreckers! Git oout with your brick in your stockin!"

Trying to Forget the Alamo

The cry of "Remember the Alamo" that was made famous by the exploits of Jim Bowie and Davie Crockett was probably not heard by Nathaniel Lewis of Falmouth.

Lewis may well have been the last living American to exit the San Antonio mission, but it was not a credit to his bravery under fire. In fact, he apparently strategically removed himself from the mission fort just before the battle, muttering something to the effect that "I am not a fighting man."

Lewis had moved west from Cape Cod in the 1820s and had become an adventurer in the Mexican state of Texas. Along with his adventuring spirit came also a reputation for making money. He settled in San Antonio and opened a store on the main plaza. By 1832 nearly everyone in the growing town owed him money. Apparently business always came first with Nathaniel Lewis. One biographer said of him, "He never let friendliness interfere with his pursuit of the dollar."

When Santa Anna's forces marched into view in February of 1836, Lewis quickly judged the odds of the coming fight and decided that he wanted no part of it. Gathering up as much of his stock as possible, he lit out to the east and safety.

When the Mexican War ended, Lewis returned to San Antonio where he lived for the rest of his life. A man of considerable wealth, he eventually became known as the "Cattle King of Texas." Lewis died on October 21, 1872 and despite earlier generous gifts of land to the city, there appears to be at least a hint of resentment in his obituary concerning his non-actions at the battle for the Alamo. His obituary, as printed in the *San Antonio Express*, read, "There are many old Texans who will miss his stalwart, positive form of manners, but the present generation will hardly find any footprints over which they may linger in reverence..."

The Harwich Killer

There is a killer in Harwich Center!

Most people entering Brooks Park miss the source of at least two violent deaths and a number of serious injuries. The killer is the old Harwich cannon.

There are actually two cannons mounted at the park's entrance across the street from the library. Each is a bit different and they don't have any identifying marks to give witness to their history. One weapon is short-barreled with a wide bore. The other is a longer gun that looks something like one of the cannons that were part of George Washington's siege of British-occupied Boston. It is this cannon that can be labeled as "the killer."

A veteran of the War of 1812 period, it is thought that the old "long Tom," as it was called, has always been a part of Harwich's history. In the early part of the eighteenth century the cannon was fired on ceremonial occasions. At that time it was located near the Brooks Academy building in Harwich Center.

In 1843, the cannon claimed its first victim when a premature discharge of the gun cost local resident Cyrus Allen the sight of one eye. Twenty years later, on July 4th 1863, while attempting to fire a salute to celebrate the Union victory at Gettysburg, a group of three youths were seriously injured when the cannon misfired. One of these boys, Edwin L. Chase, was blinded permanently in both eyes.

But it was on April 8, 1865 that the old cannon took its most devastating toll of young lives. News of the end of the Civil War

The "Harwich Killer" is the cannon in the foreground ... responsible for the deaths of two local boys, while severely injuring five others. (A. Sheedy photo)

reached Harwich and brought on wild celebrations. A number of Harwich men, most of whom were old enough to know better, dragged the cannon from its position on Parallel Street. Their intention, as stated by a contemporary writer, was "to fire a green cedar plug to Harwichport."

Shouting and whooping, the men put a four-pound double charge of gunpowder into the weapon and began to pack it with a wooden ramrod. The pressure on the old ramrod caused it to break and one of the men went into a nearby barn to get a steel crowbar to serve as a substitute. The action of the new steel ramrod set off a spark that caused the cannon to discharge. Joshua Robbins, who was standing almost in front of the muzzle, lost both of his arms below the elbows and sustained internal injuries from which he bled to death two hours later. James Baker, a recently returned Civil War veteran, was so badly burned that he did not survive the night. Ironically, Baker had survived the test of actual war service, and was killed by an innocent prank only a few hundred feet from his own house.

Benjamin F. Robbins, a survivor of the blast, took almost a year to recover from the shock. More than a month after the event he made the following notation in his journal: "Six weeks ago today, the great accident occurred which sent Joshua Robbins and James Baker into the 'upper spheres' and came near sending me there too. So near that I, at the time of the accident and again during my sickness, thought there was little chance for recovery. But I am here though I am not strong and I have a sore on my side as big as a dollar which refuses to heal and which is puffed out with proud flesh quite full."

For a number of years after, youths from Harwich Center and Harwichport vied with each other to see who could steal the cannon from one village to another. Occasional attempts were even made to fire it, although without incident. Finally, fearful that some of these youthful adventures might bring a repeat of earlier tragedies, the town fathers appropriated $13 in 1913 to bring the cannon to Brooks Park. There the killer was mounted on a cement base next to its unrelated sister – forever immobilized, unnoticed, and harmless to this day.

America's First Vietnam War Started by Cape Codder!

Captain John Percival of West Barnstable was one of the most colorful men to have ever come from this peninsula. Known as "Mad Jack" or "Roaring Jack" by his contemporaries, Percival's life included service in the War of 1812, during which he distinguished himself in capturing the British sloop *Eagle*. In a daring plan aboard an old fishing boat, his forces surprised and overcame the English captain when ordered to come along side. For that exploit, he earned his nickname. For the remainder of the war he served as a sailing master aboard a blockade-runner.

In the post-war years he commanded the first American warship to visit the Hawaiian Islands where, in 1826, he crossed swords with the missionaries who had recently arrived there. It seems that Percival didn't like the prudish taboos that the missionary societies were introducing to the natives and he urged relaxation of the new moral codes, particularly as they related to the fraternization of Hawaiian women with his sailors. His confrontation with the missionaries was not popular at home and it eventually led him to a Naval Court of Inquiry in 1828 where he was found innocent though damaged in reputation.

Captain Percival knocked around for the next decade in a series of minor commands and considered retirement. He was inactive due to ill health for several years and returned in 1841 as a Commodore. In October of 1843, in what was a surprise to many, the 64-year old sailor was given command of the venerable *U.S.S. Constitution*. After supervising its reconditioning, Percival was ordered to take the warship on an around-the-world cruise.

During the two-year voyage, *Constitution* visited many ports. On the first of May in 1845, the ship anchored off the port of Tourane, now Da Nang in the present Republic of Vietnam. At that time, Vietnam was controlled by China and Percival once again found himself involved in an issue related to Christian missionaries. The Portuguese and French had begun to send Catholic priests into what was known as Cochin China and there was a sizable Christian community there. The Chinese authorities were not happy with what they saw as growing "barbarian influence" and they arrested French Bishop Dominique Lefevre and were holding him under sentence of death.

This monument to Captain John "Mad Jack" Percival rests outside the West Barnstable cemetery at the corner of routes 6A and 149. (J. Sheedy)

Captain Percival, confidently overestimating his military power to move the local officials (a mistake that was later repeated a century later by American military commanders), threatened to blow up the local fortress and town unless the Bishop was freed. He took some Chinese officials hostage and waited for what he expected to be a parlay. These "gunboat diplomacy" tactics had worked for Percival in many of the small Pacific islands that he visited on other cruises. The standoff in Vietnam, however, continued during much of the month of May amid heat, boredom, and rising tension. The Chinese governor refused to even talk with the American commander.

Neither threats nor bribes impressed the Vietnamese. Finally, the frustrated captain released the hostages and departed the harbor without the Bishop, firing a few cannonballs at an outlying island during his exit.

This military fiasco was a major embarrassment to the United States and to the U.S. Navy. Percival's bungling of the Bishop Lefevre affair most likely hastened the end of his naval career. But his advancing age and deteriorating health, coupled with the failure to secure the post of commander of the Boston Navy Yard, was just as much a part of his decision to leave the Navy in 1849.

Percival's last years were peaceful and spent largely in Dorchester where he died in September of 1862 at the age of 83. His well-attended funeral was held in Dorchester and he is buried with an impressive marker in the village of his birth in the West Barnstable cemetery on Route 6A.

The Wellfleet Oysterman

When Henry David Thoreau came to Cape Cod in the middle of the nineteenth century he was intent on studying both the natural and the social landscape of the place. His stay in Wellfleet at the home of John Young Newcomb opened his eyes to the sort of characters that inhabited Cape Cod. The naturalist memorialized him as "The Wellfleet Oysterman."

While attempting to keep his host's tobacco spittings from landing on his breakfast as it warmed by the hearth, Thoreau listened to Newcomb's many stories. The Wellfleet man claimed that he was 14 years old at the start of the American Revolution and from his home on Williams Pond had heard the boom of cannons from Bunker Hill across Cape Cod Bay – a distance of some 60 miles!

The old man confided to Thoreau that his personal battles to control his own household had been largely unsuccessful and he allowed that he was now pretty much resigned to his fate of old age, noting "I am a poor, good-for-nothing crittur, as Isaiah says: I am all broken down this year. I am under petticoat government here." He added that he saw his elderly wife and daughter as "good-for-nothing critturs" as well.

When Thoreau returned to Wellfleet on another visit he found that Mr. Newcomb had died on December 15, 1856 at age 94. The Wellfleet oysterman rests next to the two other "critturs" (curiously, both with the name "Thankful") in the Duck Creek Cemetery on the east side of Route 6 in Wellfleet Center.

Chapter 3

Local Characters – Quirky, Courageous & Colorful

During the nineteenth century many Cape Cod skippers were involved in the China trade. Captain Alpheus Baker Jr. of South Dennis made a trip to the Orient just after the Civil War as master of the bark *Charles E. Leary*. Along with him were his wife Sarah and their children.

While in Hong Kong, the Bakers engaged the services of a Chinese woman to look after their youngsters while they took care of business and viewed the attractions of the British colony. When it came time for the family to depart China for the return trip home, the Bakers prevailed on the Chinese woman to accompany them back to Cape Cod as a caregiver for the children.

Once back in South Dennis, the Baker family settled back into the familiar routine of relatives, friends, and social activities. But for the young Chinese woman the move to America was like a transfer to another planet. In what must have been a very difficult time for her, the woman did her best to adjust to an alien culture, but homesickness and isolation contributed to the deterioration of her mental and physical health. Despite the care given to her by the Bakers, she slowly wasted away, no doubt longing for a return to her own home. It was not to be. On April 5, 1872, at the estimated age of 31, the young Chinese woman died, and was buried in a grave behind the Congregational Church. The marker simply says "Chinese Woman." She had never even been given a name!

Cape Cod is brimming with such tales of people both local and not so local. Here we present some stories of characters that serve to paint Cape Cod in a colorful, and sometimes quirky palette.

This headstone remembers a woman who died very far from home. (J. Coogan photo)

Constance Hopkins Snow – Pilgrim Woman at Nauset

There is a certain undeniable pride one feels when contemplating the plight, courage, and success of the *Mayflower* Pilgrims. Sickness took its toll on the settlers, as it was reported that, "in three months past dies halfe our company." One Pilgrim girl who survived that first terrible winter at Plimoth to later settle at Nauset was 13-year old Constance Hopkins, daughter of Pilgrim Stephen Hopkins.

In Plimoth on June 1, 1627, at the age of 20, Constance married Nicholas Snow, born in 1599 at Huxton, England. Snow had arrived at Plimoth in 1623 aboard the ship *Anne*. The couple went on to have 13 children from 1628 through 1648.

Meanwhile, in August 1638, Plimoth issued a court order allowing Constance's father to "erect a house at Mattacheese, and cut hay to winter his cattle, provided it be not to withdraw him from the Town of Plimoth." As stipulated in the court order, Hopkins' house at Mattacheese was not to be a permanent settlement. This first home built in the area by an Englishman was located near the corner of Mill Lane and Route 6A and was later sold to an Andrew Hallet, Jr. Permanent settlement of the town of Yarmouth commenced in 1639, and amongst those arriving in March of that year was Constance's brother Giles Hopkins. He went on to marry Catherine Wheldon in October 1639.

Stephen Hopkins died in 1644. That same year Constance and her family relocated to Nauset, later known as Eastham. They, along with six other families, had received permission from Governor William Bradford to relocate from Plimoth to the lower Cape. From these humble beginnings, and their offspring, came the Snows that populate the town of Orleans over 350 years later.

Constance was the only *Mayflower* Pilgrim amongst these first comers to Nauset. She was later joined by Pilgrims Joseph Rogers in 1647 and her brother Giles and his family in 1659. Giles' homestead was located along Tonset Road in Orleans. Nicholas Snow died in 1676, followed by Constance the following year, on October 25, 1677 at about the age of 70. Her grave is located at Old Cove Cemetery in Eastham, as is the grave of her brother, Giles, who departed this

earth in 1690 at around age 80. They were truly two legendary
figures from Cape Cod's past that helped tame this wild frontier.

The Importance of Being Otis

The town of Barnstable claims two important spokespersons for
American Independence in James Otis, Jr., "The Patriot," and his
sister Mercy Otis Warren.

The Otis family was a prominent force in both pre and post-
Revolutionary War activity. One member of the family played a role
in George Washington's inauguration as the first president of the
nation. In fact, Washington could not have taken office without him.

In 1740, Samuel Allyne Otis was born into eighteenth-century
Barnstable's most important family, a family with roots that
stretched back to Barnstaple, England, the namesake for Barnstable, Massachusetts. Otis' earliest ancestors in the New World
arrived at Hingham, Massachusetts in 1635 before relocating to
nearby Scituate. His great-grandfather, John Otis, arrived at West
Barnstable around 1667. His grandfather, also named John, was a
judge and a militia commander.

The youngest son of Colonel James and Mary Otis, Samuel's
siblings included James - one of the Colonies' first and most
influential patriots; Joseph - a Revolutionary War general; and
Mercy – a political satirist, a friend to John Adams and Thomas
Jefferson, and the first American to write a history of the revolutionary period. They were clearly Cape Cod's first family, 200 years
before the Kennedys came on the scene.

While brother James was making stirring revolutionary speeches
and writing anti-British pamphlets during the 1760s, Samuel gradu-
ated from Harvard and then made a name for himself as a successful
businessman. In 1764, he married Elizabeth Gray; their son Harrison
Gray Otis would go on to become the first mayor of Boston.

In 1769, Samuel's brother James was beaten by British customs
officers. The attack left the Patriot with a severe head injury and as
a result he was judged a lunatic. Samuel was named his guardian
in 1771 and was charged with the dubious task of watching over
his older brother. Many times James would sneak away and on one

occasion, it is claimed, found himself at the Battle of Bunker Hill, on June 17, 1775.

Although business prospered for Samuel throughout the 1760s, the economy of the Revolutionary War period and his willingness to extend credit began to take its toll. Despite his famous name and family connections, he fell on hard economic times and his merchant business failed. By 1785, at the age of 45, Otis declared bankruptcy. He was also unsuccessful in securing an elected position as a representative from Massachusetts in the new federal Congress. Within two years, though, he successfully reinvented himself, and with his political clout managed to get himself appointed as the first Secretary to the United States Senate. There he found his true calling, for it was a post he would hold for the remainder of his life.

During his second month in the position he performed perhaps the most important duty of his career, a duty that placed him for a few moments at the crossroads of American history. On inauguration day on April 30, 1789, in the city of New York, Samuel Otis held a red plush cushion on which lay the Bible that George Washington placed his hand upon as he took the oath of office. Not bad for a fellow who declared bankruptcy just four years earlier!

That he excelled in other examples of "political cushion holding" can be seen in Otis's use of the office of Secretary to the Senate to rebuild his financial fortunes. Because he had inside knowledge of the economic plans of the new government to assume and retire all state debts, Otis was able to gather a group of friends who began to purchase bonds at high discounts. He knew that the government planned to pay off these bonds at par value. Thus as a speculator, Otis and his friends profited greatly when the Bank of the United States paid off the bonds at full value.

Otis would go on to serve throughout the terms of Washington, Adams, Jefferson, and into Madison's second term – a total of 25 years of service. His tenure ended on April 22, 1814 in Washington where he died at the age of 74.

Cinderella was a Cape Codder!

For quite a few years a local instructor taught a short unit on

Cape Cod history to third grade students. He would show them pictures of what Cape Cod used to be like in centuries past. The students' enthusiasm was high and they were always excited by the stories that their teacher told them. This is the age where every youngster has found at least ten arrowheads, where buried treasure is hidden near old stonewalls, and at least one great grandfather was a sea captain.

One year, after doing some research in old Cape cemeteries, the teacher told the kids that he had discovered the curious fact that Cinderella had actually lived on Cape Cod. After the initial statement that "Cinderella was a Cape Codder," he watched their wide-eyed reaction and then showed them a picture of the gravestone of Cinderella Cole, a nineteenth century resident of South Wellfleet. They got a kick out of that.

In one particular class, however, the teacher noticed that when he announced that Cinderella had been a local person, one little girl didn't seem all that impressed. He asked her what she was thinking and she told him right up front.

"That's not such a big deal," she said. "Snow White lived here, too!"

When the teacher asked her to tell him more, she swore that she saw the gravestone of Snow White near her home in Dennis.

Snow White was a Cape Codder, too! (J. Sheedy photo)

"It's in the Dennis cemetery behind the fire station," she assured him. "We see it every time we walk through on the way to the library."

Intrigued by what she told him, the teacher made the effort to track the marker down. You can see by the picture that she was indeed correct.

"A Bigger Set of Rascals"

Cape Codders have always taken justifiable pride in the out-standing reputation of homegrown sailors who represented the peninsula around the world. But just as no group of people can claim immunity from at least some mischief among its ranks, so do we occasionally find a story about Cape Cod sailors who strayed from the righteous path.

Charles Tyng, who hailed from Newburyport, Massachusetts, served as a crewman aboard the ship *Suffolk* on a voyage to China in 1817. He kept a journal during the trip and noted that most of the ship's crew had been recruited from Cape Cod. They appeared to be, as he described them, "a steady set of men" and the captain gave them liberties aboard ship that reflected a confidence in their skills and integrity. Outwardly, they certainly seemed to be a model crew. On Sundays, after religious services, Tyng recorded that the Cape men spent their off hours reading or singing psalm tunes. During the normal workday, these sons of the Cape prac-ticed navigation with their quadrants and kept their journals full of information related to improving their seamanship.

The *Suffolk's* supply of spirits consisted of two barrels of rum that were lashed to the main mast in a sealed compartment just below the main deck. Unbeknownst to the captain, the crew figured out a way to tap the barrels from above by putting their quill pens together to form a long straw. In between the psalm singing, when the captain and mates were below or occupied with a task, the men inserted the pieced together straw through a gimlet hole in the head of the barrel, eventually sucking both casks dry. They used this method to also drain some wine casks that were being transported as cargo as well as to pilfer the personal supply of cherry rum that was consigned to Mr.

John Cushing, the ship's representative in Macao.

At some point in the voyage an inspection revealed what the crew was up to. The captain called all hands on deck and angrily addressed the crew, calling them "damned scoundrels."

"I sent down to Cape Cod to get a steady set of men," he shouted. "But if I had raked hell with a fine tooth comb I could not have got a bigger set of rascals."

Fortunately, the captain's anger was short lived and although their daily allowance of grog was stopped for the rest of the voyage, the crew suffered no great consequences for their action. Suffice it to say that when the captain of the *Suffolk* was looking to sign up sailors for his next voyage, he did his recruiting from Cape Ann, not from Cape Cod!

The Girl Who Was Named For a Shipwreck

The sea has always played a role in naming places on Cape Cod. Every town has a Surf Drive or an Ocean Street. The ocean has even played a part in naming youngsters from this area. Children who were born at sea were often given the middle name "Seaborne" to indicate the briny origin of their arrival into this world.

The youngsters of whalers were occasionally referred to as "Little Bowheads" and if the birth took place off a set of well-known islands such as the Marquesas, Moluccas, or the Galapagos, the place name might well also figure in the child's name. But one of the most unusual names that came as a result of the actions of the sea concerns a Cape Cod girl who was named for a nineteenth century shipwreck.

In January of 1857, the full rigged 650-ton ship *Orissa*, captained by Joshua Sears of Dennis, was driven up on Nauset Beach during a winter storm. The ship was bound for Boston from Calcutta with a cargo of gunny cloth and linseed. The particular winter season had been one of the worst in memory and many ships were lost. The bay was completely frozen from Provincetown to Brewster and newspapers recorded 18-foot snowdrifts across Cape Cod. In the middle of this terrible season the *Orissa* became a casualty of the Atlantic beach.

Eastham's Captain Dean Gray Linnell headed the volunteer surf and rescue team that came to the aid of the stricken vessel. Three crewmembers and the first mate of the *Orissa* were lost as the ship wallowed in the surf. When the survivors were taken off the hulk, Captain Linnell brought Captain Sears to his home to warm up. Only 10 days earlier, Captain Linnell and his wife Mehitable had welcomed a baby girl into their family; their seventh child. The baby still did not have a name and Captain Sears suggested that she be given the name of his ship. Thus the girl became Orissa Sears Linnell.

In gratitude for the rescue of himself and his crew, Captain Sears made a practice of regularly remembering little Orissa with gifts throughout her lifetime. Sadly, she became blind from a severe childhood illness and she never married, dying at a young age. It is one of the more curious facts of Cape Cod that with the many shipwrecks along the treacherous coastline, only one became the occasion of the name of a person - Orissa Sears Linnell.

Interestingly, some years later, the deckhouse of the *Orissa* was salvaged and dragged to South Orleans where today it is the gift shop section of the Church of the Holy Spirit.

The Man Who Never Slept

Wilbur Isaac Small of Orleans claimed to have eliminated the need for sleep by embarking on a nearly five-year marathon of sleepless days and nights between 1934 and 1939.

Born in 1871 to Isaac Kendrick and Mary McVea Small in the Barleyneck section of town, Small was a typical Cape Cod "Jack of all trades." He lived with his brother Fred and apparently never felt the urge to marry. During this time, he also seemed to lack the need to sleep, often going days without putting his head to the pillow. After hearing of a no sleep contest, something similar to the dance marathons of the time, Small decided that such an easy prize was there for the taking. He went for periods of over 80 days without sleep and culminated it in a record-breaking "all-nighter" that lasted 147 days!

In 1934, he went a full year without sleep, noting that the only thing it cost him was about 10 pounds. When this record was in the book he declared that staying awake was so easy that he would continue to defy the arms of Morpheus indefinitely. By 1937 his fame reached the big city and he was invited to New York in March for an interview with Gabriel Heatter, host of the radio program "We the People." He impressed listeners with the veracity of his strange gift and he was declared a medical marvel.

Despite the skeptical criticism of a number of Boston doctors who claimed that he was a fake, Small, who was known locally as "Bill-Ike," was never observed as even taking so much as a nap during this period. He claimed that he never used any artificial stimulants, such as tea or coffee, to stay awake. Interestingly, he noted that his brother Fred was "the soundest sleeper I ever saw."

"Bill Ike" outlasted individuals and groups that attempted to monitor his sleeplessness, and when he died on a cold January night in 1939, after apparently suffering a stroke while walking home from Orleans center, it was said that death was the only thing that could have closed his eyes.

Frank Cabral's Wild Ride

Upon a clear morning in late June of 1948, 17-year-old high school student Frank Cabral and his father took their 30-foot lobster boat out of Provincetown Harbor to a spot off Race Point to pull lobster traps. At about 8:30 a.m. the two were in separate 16-foot dories when the father looked up and spotted a good sized whale bearing down on young Frank.

Hardly a moment passed before the whale closed the 500 yards between them and briefly submerged. Suddenly the creature came up under the boy's dory, tossing it in the air. Frank was looking down at the trap line and hadn't seen the whale nor had he heard his father's brief warning shout.

The surprised youth went up about seven feet and came down directly on the back of the swimming animal. Frank was then taken for a short ride while sitting astride the whale. The father later estimated that his son had been on the whale's back for only several seconds, but the time must have seemed much longer to the stunned boy as the event unfolded.

Just as quickly as it had happened, the whale shook off the

seagoing cowboy and sounded. As Frank's father rowed quickly toward him, the boy was able to climb back into the righted dory. Although Frank's boat was sinking from a hole made by the impact of the collision, the two lobstermen were able to save the outboard motor and even the harvested lobsters. The small boat was towed back to the Cape tip and hauled out for repairs.

When word of what had happened circulated around the waterfront Frank found himself something of a celebrity. He suffered a cut finger and a bruised toe, but was otherwise un-scathed from his mini-version of a "Nantucket sleigh ride." Inspection of the damaged dory revealed a one-foot square hole where the whale struck it.

Area newspapers picked up the story of the young whale rider and Frank and his father were invited to be on the radio show, "We the People," in New York City. They were flown down and put up in the Belmont Plaza Hotel. Frank told the radio audience about his adventure with the now-named "Willie the Whale" and attributed his coolness under duress to his Boy Scout swimming training. Not long after this, Frank appeared on another radio program, "Ripley's Believe it or Not."

Frank Cabral joined the storied whaling lore of Provincetown more by accident than by intent. But his adventure was certainly unique. In the long line of his townsmen who experienced close encounters with the largest creatures of the sea, he is the only one known to have ever taken a ride on the back of a whale.

Harry's Ashes

There are lots of stories about Harry Kemp, the Provincetown Poet of the Dunes. Some called him "the last Bohemian" and "the poet of the open road." Others considered him a modern Walt Whitman. To the people of the Cape tip who knew him, especially in his later life, Harry was probably something in between.

In the tightly knit community that Provincetown was a half century ago, the town adopted him as one of their own and he responded with a passion for things connected to the place. While his poetry admittedly appealed to a somewhat narrow audience, he was always available for sales of his work at his home address. Or, as he advertised in the *Advocate*, you could stop him on the street and buy a book from him personally. He would take out a seagull feather and autograph it on the spot with his left hand!

It was said that he swam in Provincetown Harbor all year round, as long as there was an audience. At one time he reportedly "bombed" Plymouth Rock with flour sacks in retaliation for that town's continued boast that the Pilgrims landed there first. Very much an activist, he protested everything from the high price of coffee by dumping some into Provincetown harbor, to the fact that a national soap company wanted to move "wash day" from its original Pilgrim-inspired Monday.

Harry Kemp was born in 1883 in Ohio. He was four years old when his mother died and his father soon after left town. The father would be in and out of the boy's life and Harry lived much of his youth with his grandmother. He moved to New Jersey as a teenager and tried school for a while but dropped out and headed for the open road at 17 years of age. His travels over the next two years took him around the world as a worker, a stowaway, and as a friend to anyone who would take him in. It was sort of a portent of how he would live his adult life at the Cape tip.

In 1902, he was able to get himself admitted to the Northfield Mount Herman prep school where he continued to pursue unconformity and rebelliousness. He dropped out in the winter of 1904, returning briefly in 1905 only to get expelled later that year.

He ended up in Lawrence, Kansas during 1906 where he enrolled in the University of Kansas. While there he became the protégé of William Allen White and friend to social liberals like Ida Tarbell and Upton Sinclair. Later he moved to Greenwich Village in New York where he met and married his first wife Mary Pyne. They spent the summer of 1916 in Provincetown where she acted with the Province-town Players group and he worked on his poetry. Pyne was never well and she died in 1919 of tuberculosis. Despite his declarations that marriage put too many limits on his freedom, Kemp never got over it.

While living in Greenwich Village just before World War I, Kemp ran with a band of bohemians who summered in Provincetown including George Cram Cook, Edmund Wilson, Eugene O'Neil, and Jack Reed. In that first summer at the Cape tip he took out an advertisement announcing that in exchange for a cottage he would supply the landlord with works written by a "well known" poet. The writer, of course, was himself.

He fit well enough with the literati that made up the Provincetown Players, but he was reportedly never a reliable actor. He often made up his own lines when he thought that they might improve the play. Eventually he wrote over 30 one-act plays for the group though only a few were ever actually produced.

Kemp married Frances McClernan in 1924 and they summered in Provincetown where he joined the Wharf Players. In 1927, he began living summers in the dunes, occupying a shack on the backside near Peaked Hill. That same year McClernan left him and headed for Paris.

Alternating between winters in the Village and summers in Provincetown, Kemp epitomized the unorthodox lifestyle of many in the arts community there. By the 1940s he was living year-round at the Cape tip. Each spring he would vacate his in-town apartment and head for his dune shack carrying his typewriter and a stove. There he spent the summers, entertaining anyone who might happen to drop in.

Two months before his death in the summer of 1960, Kemp, a long time agnostic, converted to Roman Catholicism. He told friends that he did it as a favor for young Father Duart who, he said, could use converts of any sort. His close friends were surprised at his sudden apparent need for a formal religion, but then not much that he did shocked anyone. But when they heard that his remains were about to be embalmed and prepared for a traditional burial, his friends went into action.

Kemp's original will stipulated that he was to be cremated and his ashes scattered in Greenwich Village and the Provincetown dunes. Yet the rules of the Catholic Church did not allow cremation. His friends approached the Church for a dispensation, citing the will as evidence of how Harry would have wanted his remains to be treated. But the will was dated prior to Kemp's conversion. The Church considered it null and void.

A row began over what to do with the body. Sunny Tasha, who had built Kemp a new dune shack, and who was perhaps his closest friend, went to the mortuary and, without authorization, spirited the body to the Forest Hills crematorium. But the members of his new religious faith blocked the action claiming that Tasha had no authority to make off with Kemp's remains. Some Catholics felt that Tasha's actions would surely consign Harry's soul to Hell. They called in the state police and had the body returned to Provincetown for a proper Catholic burial ceremony.

The Welfare Committee then claimed jurisdiction over the remains in the absence of an immediate relative. Finally, Tasha was able to produce another copy of Harry's will dated four days after his conversion. Where she got it from she wasn't saying. As executrix, she again took the body off-Cape and carried out the cremation. Harry Kemp's ashes were scattered over the Provincetown Dunes in the area of his shack. About a month later, the rest of his ashes were scattered near various old haunts in Greenwich Village. He was now, as one friend observed, "where the wind blows."

Provincetown dune poet Harry Kemp, with "Sunny" Tasha, striking a rather historic pose as he reenacts the Pilgrims' first washday in the new world. (John D. Bell photo; courtesy of the William Brewster Nickerson Room Collection, Cape Cod Community College. Donors Josephine and Salvatore Del Deo)

Chapter 4

Of Tales Theological

It is almost impossible to separate the history of Cape Cod from its connection to the spiritual side of settlement. Early Cape Codders were the sons and daughters of solid Pilgrim stock and they carried their religious views with them as they spread out from Plimoth.

Religion played a key role in the establishment of new communities in the Old Colony. Ministers often led their flocks to new settlement areas and these spiritual advisors held sway over the political, economic, and social life of emerging towns. After a century of domination by the Congregationalists, a variety of different religious sects began to settle on Cape Cod. Quakers, Baptists, and Methodists were some of the first groups to challenge the old Puritan hegemony. By the nineteenth century other religious persuasions were beginning to vie for recognition and legitimacy, often creating temporary moments of discontent as the old order was forced to accommodate new ideas and challenges to orthodoxy. The pattern has continued to the present day.

The legacy of religious influence as it affects Cape Cod is present in some of the now archaic bylaws that still can be found in town codes. The so-called "Blue Laws" that still restrict certain types of business activity are traced to an earlier time when all laws had to conform to a fairly conservative and religious set of norms. The wonderful assortment of church architecture is another reflection of three centuries of the religious presence on the Cape. A few of these buildings and some of the interesting people who frequented these houses of worship are the subject of this chapter.

Yarmouth's Worshipping Woes

Colonial records show many circumstances where ministers and members of their flock did not see eye-to-eye. Such is the case with Yarmouth's first permanent minister, Reverend Marmaduke Matthews, and certain members of his fledgling congregation.

Matthews, who was among the first settlers of the town in 1639, was born at Swansey in the county of Glamonshire, Wales in 1605 and was educated at Oxford. He was an intelligent man with a sharp wit, yet with ideals and an apparent lack of discretion that did not rest well with those about him. While in his mid-twenties, Matthews and his wife Katherine left their home in Barnstaple, England, arriving in the New World sometime between 1628 and 1630 aboard the ship *Brevis*. Their Yarmouth home rested near the new meetinghouse in roughly the center of town.

Almost immediately his ministry was attacked by church member William Chase. Arriving in the New World in 1630, and appointed Yarmouth constable in 1639, it is believed that Chase, his wife Mary and three children were members of the failed 1638 settlement led by Reverend Stephen Bachiler. Chase made repeated derogatory statements against Reverend Matthews, notably saying that he "marvelled how any durst joyne with him in the fast." He was hauled into Plimoth Court and was subsequently relieved of his constable position.

During the very next year Chase was at it again, verbally assaulting Reverend Matthews and disrupting church service. Again he found himself in court where he was censured, fined, and told to leave Yarmouth. Somehow, Chase remained in Yarmouth, and appears to have kept his comments to himself for the remaining years of Matthews' ministry.

Within a year, four other members of the community spoke out against Matthews, among them physician Thomas Tilley and William Nickerson, who would later go on to settle the town of Chatham. Acquitted by the Plimoth Court, the four men next invited Reverend Joseph Hull from neighboring Barnstable to relocate to Yarmouth and form a second church. Back they went to Plimoth Court where they were told not to "depart from the government." The Court then forbade Hull to relocate to Yarmouth and advised him to abandon his thoughts of forming a Yarmouth church otherwise risk arrest. Excommunicated from the Barnstable church, Hull was later reinstated although he eventually left town, moving to New Hampshire.

In the wake of all this, the Court began to take a closer look at Reverend Matthews, although Governor Winthrop referred to him as "a goodly minister." He was cited for "weak and unsafe expressions in his teaching." Of the four complaining church members, all but Tilley eventually left Yarmouth, as did Reverend Matthews about 1645, relocating (ironically) to the town of Hull, and then to Malden before finally returning to Wales where his ministry continued to attract controversy until his death in 1683.

Thumpertown

Along with resident ministers that set the fur flying with blazing sermons came the nineteenth century practice of establishing summertime religious camp meetings where whole groups of Cape Codders could combine good sermonizing with outdoor socializing.

Wellfleet began its Camp Meeting Week in 1819 and attracted enthusiastic worshippers. Cottage City, now Oak Bluffs on Martha's Vineyard, served the same purpose on that island. In Harwichport, the Cape Cod Association of Spiritualists met each summer during much of the late nineteenth century at what is still called "Ocean Grove."

Eastham Methodists established an outdoor center for evangelism at "Millennium Grove" in North Eastham in 1828. People came from all over to absorb an atmosphere where, as one writer put it, "God's glory cloud of grace filled the place and made it a sanctuary of holy things." Yarmouth had its Methodist campground about a mile from the railroad depot off Willow Street that brought in sinners by the train carload for summer revivalism.

Others looked at the same scenes and beheld a different message. Writer Henry David Thoreau commented that some 150 ministers and up to 5,000 hearers assembled in the grove for what seemed to him a sort of spiritual clambake. "A man is appointed to clear out the pump a week beforehand, while the ministers are clearing their throats; but probably, the latter do not always deliver as pure a stream as the former," he wrote, after observing a revival meeting on one of his visits to Cape Cod in the 1850s.

That not everyone who attended these religious assemblies was filled with the spirit of repentance can also be seen in a Boston newspaper story about the arrest of several pickpockets, card sharks, and tricksters, along with some of the money they had fleeced from gullible attendees.

Up to three sermons were preached each day in the grove. The fervor that accompanied the prayer services caused many to move in a spiritual frenzy. "Old time" religion even left its mark in the form of an Eastham place name. The section of town known as "Thumpertown" seems to have come from actions of the preachers who would emphasize strong points with enthusiastic Bible references, banging the Holy Book on the pulpit to drive the lesson home, hence the name "thumpers." Eventually the spirit died out and Millennium Grove was abandoned in 1863.

The Barefooted Quaker

Along Main Street in the quiet village of Cotuit rests the historic Samuel Dottridge Homestead. The building, originally built in Harwich about 1790, was owned by a widow named Abigail Chase. The Cape Cod-style homestead consisted of a parlor and bedroom flanking the front entrance, with the keeping room at the rear running the length of the house. The dwelling was not originally built as a full Cape, but was enlarged at some later date.

A mother of three, Abigail met a young man named Samuel Benjamin Dottridge, who at the time was an apprentice cabinetmaker in Brewster working for a John Baker of that town. Dottridge had been born in England in 1786 and arrived on Cape Cod in his teenage years just after the turn of the nineteenth century. After his apprenticeship was concluded, Dottridge married Abigail around 1807 or 1808. About 1811 they relocated to Cotuit, bringing their house along with them, pulled behind a team of oxen!

A Quaker, Dottridge traveled by foot to church service at the Quaker Meetinghouse in Barnstable each Sabbath. It was believed he walked to the meetinghouse because, being a Quaker, it was forbidden to ride a horse on the Sabbath. Also, it is said that he would walk the many miles barefooted, carrying his shoes because he did not want to wear them out.

Abigail, who was born in 1777, died in 1848. Dottridge remarried two years later and moved to East Sandwich, this time leaving his home behind. He died in 1855 at the age of 68 years. As for the homestead, it remained in the Dottridge family into the mid-twentieth century when it became the home of the Santuit-Cotuit Historical Society, holding that distinction to this day.

Yet, casting back some two centuries it is not difficult to imagine the village as it once was, with salt works along the shore and oyster shacks down on Cotuit Bay. In the air, the sound of hammering from the local cooperage, supplying barrels for both industries.

And it is not difficult to imagine a shoeless Quaker off in the distance, walking the long miles to church, in touch with some higher purpose.

When Lightning Strikes

Among the oldest congregational churches in the state, the First Congregational Church of Yarmouth was organized in 1639, just prior to the town's incorporation during that same year.

It is believed that the original 30 foot by 20 foot, thatched roof

church building stood in the ancient cemetery located between
Winter and Center streets. Men sat on the east side of the church,
women on the west. A plaque on the cemetery grounds, dedicated
on September 20, 1979 at a 340th anniversary celebration, marks
the location.

The first minister in town was Reverend Marmaduke Matthews.
He was followed to the pulpit by Reverend John Miller in 1647
who was instrumental in bringing the church back together after
the schism that had occurred during the Matthews ministry.

Steeple repair at the First Congregational Church of Yarmouth. A landmark for mariners of the late 1800s, this steeple has seen much "action" over the twentieth century. (A. Sheedy photo)

Reverend Miller was succeeded by Reverend Thomas Thornton, from 1667 to 1693, who introduced a more relaxed and democratic church doctrine.

In 1716, during the ministry of Reverend Daniel Greenleaf (from 1708 to 1727), a larger church building was constructed to accommodate the growing congregation. The original building was moved to become a private residence and may have survived into the early twentieth century before it was razed. By far, the longest ministry was that of Reverend Timothy Alden, Jr., descendant of Pilgrim John Alden, who served the community from 1769 to 1828. During his tenure the east parish of Yarmouth separated amicably from the town to become incorporated as the township of Dennis.

Following Alden was Reverend Nathaniel Cogswell, whose ministry from 1828 to 1851 saw the building of a new church edifice along what is today Old Church Street in Yarmouthport, where the playground in now located. Forty years later, in 1870, the present church on Zion Hill was constructed with its massive 135-foot steeple serving as a landmark for mariners at sea.

The building on Old Church Street later became a post office and burned in 1902. As for the current church, its steeple has seen much activity over the years, toppling in hurricanes during the 1940s and 1950s and was at least on one occasion struck by lightning.

Another church to be struck by lightning was the Universalist meetinghouse on Main Street in Hyannis. On July 7, 1871, a thunderstorm rumbled across Cape Cod. From that summer storm leapt a bolt of lightning, setting the church ablaze. The story goes that the sexton at the nearby Baptist church refused to ring his church's bell to alert the volunteer fire brigade, claiming that the bolt of lightning and the ensuing fire was "God's will." As a result, the Universalist meetinghouse, built in 1847, subsequently burned to the ground.

The Deacon Sea Captain

When considering the typical Cape Cod sea captain, images of a crusty old man with a flowing white beard and a pipe in his mouth, fighting off pirates and cursing up a storm, come to mind.

Cape Cod certainly had its share of colorful sea captains and
swashbucklers who sailed dangerous journeys to foreign ports and
were worldly in their many experiences. They were the more
flamboyant of the Cape's masters, making a name for themselves
with their tales of daring exploits.

Yet, one of Cape Cod's most esteemed sea captains was a gentle-
manly seafaring servant of God who was known to frequent
church services when he arrived at a foreign port rather than the
nearest watering hole with the rest of the sailing men. His manner
and his temperament delivered him to the loftiest commands of his
era, and immortalized him as a highly talented shipmaster as well
as a most decent person. He was the deacon sea captain Josiah
Richardson of Centerville.

Josiah's father, John Richardson, was a Harvard graduate who
became a schoolmaster. As a young man he arrived at Centerville
around 1798 to live, to work and to eventually take a wife and
raise a family. He and his wife Hannah were to produce two
prominent Cape Cod sea captains in sons Josiah and Ephraim.
Josiah became a cabin boy in 1820, at the age of 11, and nine years
later became master of the schooner *Hetty Thom*.

At age 22, the up and coming Josiah Richardson was put in charge
of the brig *Orbit*, which he sailed out of Boston in what would
become his first of many transatlantic voyages. Throughout his 20s
and into his early 30s he plied the waters of the Atlantic, sailing the
brigs *Owhyhee* and *Leander* to Marseilles, France. Occasionally he
would also sail to Brazil or to Russia. By 1839 he became master of
the vessel *Chatham*, which he sailed from southern United States
ports to Liverpool, England and Le Havre, France over the next two
years, chiefly transporting cargoes of cotton.

During the mid-1840s he was on dry land long enough to marry
and dabble in growing fruit trees, an interestingly agrarian hobby
for such a seafaring man. He also found time to serve as deacon at
the local church, a relationship with the Lord that he would carry
with him to his final day.

Back at sea in January 1847, his first passage across the Atlantic
was one to test the skill, mettle and character of the greatest of sea
captains. On what would seem a routine journey from New York

to Liverpool, his vessel *Walpole,* with a cargo of wheat, took on water. Even with the bilge pumps going the level of seawater in the ship's lower decks continued to rise. Unfortunately, the pumps were becoming clogged with wheat. Remarkably, the *Walpole* and her crew arrived at Liverpool 28 days after leaving New York, limping into port waterlogged, her cargo ruined. Thus concluded what Richardson called "an ugly cross sea running."

After repairs to his vessel, Richardson sailed for Manila later in the year, arriving at the Straits of Sunda in August after 95 days at sea. Two years later he was master of the *Townsend,* a new vessel built to run the Liverpool packet trade. This position took him to ports such as New Orleans, of which the deacon sea captain wrote to his wife: "The wicked indeed are like the troubled sea. The fruits of their lives blast and mildew on those around them, and their final end, Death Eternal. They know not the happiness of domestic bliss, mutual love, mutual happiness ... The wicked grope in the darkness; they flee where no man pursueth – there is no peace for the wicked."

His letters to his wife, as documented in Kittredge's book *The Shipmasters of Cape Cod,* paint a picture of a pious man in touch with the goodness of soul, his belief in God, and his deep love toward his wife and commitment to their long-distance relationship. From St. John's, Newfoundland he later writes: "I went to Episcopal church twice. The morning sermon, could not hear the preacher but a few words. In the evening it did much better."

The year 1850 saw the loss of his former vessel, *Walpole,* which was abandoned by her crew in the Columbia River out in the Pacific Northwest. Richardson still owned a $10,000 interest in the vessel. Upon learning of this personal monetary loss, Richardson wrote to his wife: "It's past; no murmuring. Onward to the Christian. All is well at last. Nothing comes by chance; a kind, all-wise Father over rules all accidents and miscalculations of man, showing him his weaknesses and shortsightedness and dependence."

He later told his wife not to be concerned about spending money despite their recent financial setback: "... it is best to live comfortable, if we die poor."

Yet, the deacon's luck was soon to change. It seems that good guys do finish first, as the gentleman sea captain was offered the command of ship designer Donald McKay's newest and most ambitious vessel to date. In 1850 the *Stag Hound* was launched, introducing the world to a whole new breed of clipper ship ... referred to by Mr. Kittredge as an "extreme" clipper. Her lines were such as had never been seen before. She was built for speed and some were frightened by her possibilities. Some even questioned if the greatest of sea captains could manage her, to which Captain Richardson responded, "I would not go in the ship at all if I thought for a moment she would be my coffin."

Enough said, for *Stag Hound* sailed in February 1851 for San Francisco with Captain Richardson in command. The vessel arrived there in a speedy 112 days, despite losing the main topmast and three topgallant masts in a gale on the sixth day out. And despite stopping to pick up nine survivors of the wrecked Russian ship *La Sylphide* off the coast of Brazil.

In a letter from the Russian Ambassador to Secretary of State Daniel Webster, Captain Richardson was praised for his humanity: "He fed them on board his vessel during six weeks, and after landing them at Valparaiso (Chile), Captain Richardson positively refused to receive any ... compensation whatever." He went on to say, "His Imperial Majesty has been pleased to authorize me, Mr. Secretary of State, to convey his thanks to Captain Richardson as well as to express his gratitude to that officer for the promptness with which he hastened to save and take care of these Russian sailors."

Richardson remained in command of the *Stag Hound* until a new command was offered to him in May 1852. The latest vessel was McKay's new clipper *Staffordshire*, designed to carry passengers in modern day comfort. On her maiden voyage, Richardson sailed her from Boston to San Francisco in 101 days, "the shortest of the season thus far" he reported to his wife in an August 13 letter.

The lofty captain, in command of perhaps the greatest vessel in the world, became the toast of San Francisco during his brief stay in the city. Yet, his interests in port continued to gravitate toward the spiritual. Ever the deacon, Richardson opted for Sunday school meetings over highbrow parties. He spoke to groups of children, prompting the holy of San Francisco to insist, "that I must visit all the Sabbath Schools in San Francisco." He also mentioned in a letter that, "I have had most of the Reverend Gentlemen on board the *Staffordshire*."

This peninsula produced hundreds of fine seamen, each representing Cape Cod in his own, unique way. As Cape deepwater shipmasters go, Captain Richardson was one of her most famous, and certainly one of her most pious.

Kelley Chapel

Along a woodland trail, just south of Route 6A in the village of Yarmouthport, is Kelley Chapel. This wonderful little church building was constructed by David Kelley of South Yarmouth back in 1873 and resided for much of its life in a section of that Quaker village. Its original site rested between Wood Road and Old North Main Street, not far from the Quaker Meetinghouse that still stands in that historic village.

Kelley built the chapel for his daughter, Rosa Kelley Parker, who had lost her 20-month-old son the year before. Since 1868, Rosa

The simplicity of Kelley Chapel remembers a time when Quakers populated villages across the Cape. (A. Sheedy photo)

had been reading the Bible to members of the community in private homes throughout the village, and Kelley felt that providing her with a chapel to continue her work would take her mind off the death of the young boy.

Though father and daughter were both Quakers, the chapel was non-denominational. Tragically, Rosa died one year later. Kelley carried on, and the chapel continued to host prayer readings, hymns, testimonials, and even strawberry festivals since Kelley was a strawberry grower. Visiting ministers arrived at the chapel to offer sermons, and beginning in 1904 Amos Kelley Haswell, the grandson of David Kelley, commenced his ministry there. He preached in the old Kelley chapel for over 50 years, but by 1959 the congregation was reduced to a point that the octogenarian Haswell offered the building up as a gift to the town's historical society.

The following year the building was moved from South Yarmouth to Yarmouthport where it resides today. During the mid-1960s, it was converted into a Civil War era schoolhouse museum, but was later renovated and re-opened in 1979 as a chapel. Inside are 12 simple white pews that are believed to have come from a 1714 Quaker meetinghouse that once stood near Follins Pond.

The Roller Skating Rink that Became a Church

Until the last years of the nineteenth century there was no Catholic Church in the town of Truro. Many of the Catholic Portuguese fisherman and their families who were beginning to inhabit the town and nearby Provincetown were interested in having their own place of worship. In 1895, the Enos family donated some land near the county road for the purpose of building a church.

Instead of putting up a new church, the parish decided instead to purchase an old skating rink that was located near Perry's Hill in South Truro, near Mill Pond Road. The building had started its life in 1852 as the Obadiah Brown School. Men of the parish broke the building down into sections and moved it up to Truro Center near the Town Hall. Once reassembled, the church was dedicated and put into use during the same year. Interestingly, during the first few years of its service, Sacred Heart, as the church came to be named, held all of its services in Portuguese, the only church on Cape Cod to ever do so.

The Church that Came in From the Sea

The main street of Buzzards Bay today leaves visitors with a sense that the high tide of prosperity must have occurred there many years ago. There is not much happening. The wrack line of activity that remains is pretty much confined to convenience stores, faded buildings, and second hand shops.

But in June of 1947, the tide brought in something that many villagers had dreamt of and worked toward for years. And it was something that today continues to add a touch of beauty to Buzzards Bay. The high tide brought in Saint Peter's Episcopal Church.

The story of how this church came ashore begins with the arrival in 1944 of the Episcopal Reverend John Stephenson to a small mission parish that was organized in Buzzards Bay about eight years earlier. The congregation had no church of its own and was using a fraternal lodge for services. Father Stephenson was posted to the upper Cape as a "missioner" and his territory also included St. John's Church in Sandwich. He realized that if the Buzzards Bay parish was ever to grow and prosper it needed its own building of worship.

For several years, the priest looked for ways to house his flock in a permanent church. When Camp Edwards closed up at the end of World War II, he tried unsuccessfully to purchase one of the base chapels so that it could be moved to Buzzards Bay. A building fund was established in hopes that something could someday be constructed.

About this time, Father Stephenson got wind of an available church building that was located up the coast in Hull, Massachusetts. The building was the Church of Our Savior in the Allerton section of the town. It had not been used for a number of years and he was told that he could have it if he could move it. Unfortunately, the cost of moving the building 45 miles down the highway to Buzzards Bay was more than the amount of funds available.

Undaunted, Father Stephenson investigated the possibility of
shipping the building to Buzzards Bay on a barge. The numbers
were favorable and in late May the church was ready for transport.

The actual arrival of the building did not take place until early
June as the move awaited favorable tides and winds to make the
60-mile sea voyage. Many watched along the canal as the little
church followed in the wake of the tugboat *Bounty*. Once under the
Bourne Bridge and the Railroad Bridge, the barge was made fast to
some pilings just to the south of Main Street.

Yet, at the last minute there was a slight hitch. The supervisor for
the Cape and Vineyard Electric Company told the moving crews
that he wouldn't authorize the moving of any wires because all of
the proper permits hadn't been completed. Father Stephenson was
worried because the building couldn't be insured until it was set
on its foundation. Time was of the essence. Before it became a
crisis, someone persuaded the supervisor that he was needed
elsewhere in Plymouth County. While he was out of town, some
off-duty linemen moved the wires and the building was lined up
to make the 500-yard transfer across open land to the church
property. With winches and rollers, the building was moved to its
present location where it was set on a permanent foundation.

Like the rock of its namesake, Saint Peter's on-the-Canal had
come permanently home to its congregation.

Chapter 5

A Seafaring Past

When the famous Cape Cod novelist Joseph C. Lincoln talked about Brewster, the town of his birth, he said that just about every man that he knew there, as a child, with the exception perhaps of the minister, became a sea captain. While that may have been something of an exaggeration, the fact is that Cape Cod produced a great number of men, and even a few women, who made their mark on the waters that washed along the peninsula.

Hundreds of "coastermen" ran schooners along the east coast, hauling cargos from Maine to Florida. There wasn't a house in the village that didn't have at least one male member at sea either in the fisheries or in the merchant trade for some period of time. Some of the best of these mariners became legends in the great age of sail, driving clipper ships to records in both the Atlantic and Pacific Oceans. To be a "Cape Cod Blue Water Man" was to hold a rank of distinction among a worldwide fraternity of seagoing adventurers and entrepreneurs.

The ships and the men who commanded them have become part of the wonderful lore and history of Cape Cod. Their achievements seem almost mythical as we look back to an age when a trip around Cape Horn was almost as common as a modern-day trip to the mall. From Bombay to Brazil, the reputation of Cape Cod was carried by her sea captains, and it was no small wonder that historian Henry C. Kittredge said that the greatest of them "became the aristocrats of an already aristocratic profession - the conquerors of the conquerors of the world."

Eluding History

Orleans was home to the eighteenth century sea captain who, it seems, may or may not have been the first American shipmaster to circumnavigate the globe.

Born in Harwich in 1740, Captain John Kendrick made a name for himself during the Revolutionary War commanding privateers. He seemed just the type of sea captain Boston merchants had in mind to open up a fur trade route to the Northwest since Britain, to the northeast, was boycotting American goods in the wake of the war.

In 1787, Kendrick set off from Boston in the 83-foot, 250-ton *Columbia,* along with the sloop *Lady Washington*, commanded by Lieutenant Robert Gray. The plan was to round Cape Horn, obtain furs in the Northwest, sail to China to trade the furs for silk, and then voyage home via the Cape of Good Hope, thus circumnavigating the globe. The voyage, if successful, would make Kendrick the first American commander to sail around the world.

Yet, Kendrick found a way to elude his place in the history books. From the start his heart appeared not to be into his work. Before rounding the Horn he spent a month at the Cape Verde Islands and another 10 days at the Falklands. Arriving along the Pacific coast around 1788, he sent Gray off in the *Columbia* to secure a cargo of furs while he built a home for himself on Vancouver Island. In the process, Gray claimed discovery of the Columbia River, which he named for his vessel. He most likely also was one of the first explorers to visit nearby Gray River and Gray's Harbor.

Kendrick then placed Gray in command of the *Columbia* to sail for China and complete the voyage. "At this point the Captain's character began to disintegrate," writes Kittredge in his book *Cape Cod – Its People and Their History*. He spent the remainder of his life as a fur trader, journeying between Vancouver Island and Hawaii. He did manage to reach China on at least two occasions, but for the most part he remained in the Northwest where he became surprisingly effective in bartering with the Native Indians for sea otter pelts.

He was killed at Hawaii around 1793 or 1794 in a freak accident during a cannon salute with a British vessel. Unfortunately the British cannon was loaded and aimed right at Kendrick. There are some reports that Kendrick (spelled in most Cape history books as *Kenrick*) returned to South Orleans in 1792 to build a home. Yet other information shows that the house may have been built around 1780 or just after the Revolutionary War.

Most sources today cite Robert Gray as the "American explorer" who discovered the Columbia River, and not the "fur trader" Kendrick. In fact, the first explorer to reach the Columbia River was British Captain James Cook who visited Nootka Sound almost 10 years earlier, in 1778.

As an aside, NASA named its first space shuttle *Columbia* after the eighteenth century vessel.

Cape Cod's Sea Captain "Prince"

One Dennis ship captain who went on to become a successful clipper ship owner was Prince S. Crowell of East Dennis. Born in 1813 at the height of the war with Britain, he went to sea at a young age and by his early twenties had already achieved the position of master of the schooner *Soldam*, and later the schooner *Edwin*. By age 26 he was in command of a third schooner, *Deposit*, on which he made transatlantic voyages to Europe, and in the case of his 1839 voyage, to Palermo, Sicily.

Though other Dennis shipmasters battled the waters of Cape Horn toward Pacific destinations, Crowell spent most of his career in the Atlantic servicing European ports. In the 1840s he was in command of the *Aurelius*, moving cargoes of tobacco from Richmond, Virginia to Liverpool, England. He also transported cotton from southern ports to Europe on the bark *Autoleon*. He did

(Inset) Ship captain and ship owner Prince S. Crowell. (William Brewster Nickerson Room Collection - Cape Cod Community College) and the grave marker of Captain Prince S. Crowell. (A. Sheedy photo)

venture to China in 1846 as master of the *Thomas W. Sears* with a cargo of tobacco, fish and tools, receiving $100 per month in pay for his efforts.

Along with fellow East Dennis ship captain Christopher Hall, in 1849 he provided financial support to the brothers Shiverick for the construction of their shipyard. When Hall died in 1857, Crowell became Dennis' chief ship owner. Crowell himself died a wealthy man in 1881, as his large polished marble monument at the East Dennis village cemetery will attest.

Steaming to the Islands – Nineteenth Century Style

Nowadays, a sojourn to the islands of Nantucket and Martha's Vineyard on board any of the modern day ferries operating out of Hyannis, Woods Hole, or Falmouth Harbor seems a common, everyday event. The vessels leave port on schedule and arrive at their destination on time, with a safe and comfortable passage in between. A trip by sea to Nantucket from Hyannis takes exactly two hours. A new high-speed vessel can cut an hour off the commute.

Yet, prior to 1818, the popular way to reach the islands of Nantucket and Martha's Vineyard was via any of the packets departing from a number of south side Cape Cod ports. These packets were quite dependable, were commanded by experienced masters and crews, and provided an important link between the "far away" lands and the mainland. They delivered passengers, freight, and the mail. Their passages were plagued by rough seas, head winds, and heavy ice. Packets remained in service throughout much of the nineteenth century, but technology eventually rendered them obsolete.

Competition first appeared in 1818 when a 100-ton, 90-foot steam-powered paddleboat christened *Eagle* arrived at New Bedford to provide service to Nantucket Island. Built the year before, it was the latest state-of-the-art steam vehicle, spinning off of Robert Fulton's invention some 10 years earlier. Considered the first New England-based steamboat to provide anything closely resembling "regular service," the *Eagle* made her first passage in

May of that year. By September she ended her short run as passengers to the island still preferred the reliable packets to the sometimes dangerous steam-driven vehicles (on her inaugural run off Connecticut during the previous year the *Eagle's* boiler had blown up!). Similar explosions on other steamboats were all too common at that time, resulting in the injuries and deaths of hundreds of passengers each year.

Even with her steam power, the *Eagle* was never able to break the eight-hour mark in her passages to Nantucket. About a dozen years after leaving Buzzards Bay the vessel was wrecked off the coast of Maine.

In the meantime, other steamboats would attempt to make a profit transporting passengers and freight to Nantucket. The vessel *Connecticut*, at 150-feet, arrived in 1824 and made the run for about four years, followed almost immediately by the 60-ton *Hamilton*, originally named *LaFayette*. In fact, although the name *Hamilton* appeared over her paddlewheels, her former name of *LaFayette* appeared prominently at her stern. This latest vessel not only possessed an identity crisis but also a fiscal crisis, as she was unable to turn a profit. After only a few months in operation she ended her island service. Her fate matched that of the *Eagle* as she, too, was wrecked off the coast of Maine seven years after leaving Buzzards Bay.

Yet another steamer arrived to take the *Hamilton's* place. That vehicle was the *Marco Bozzaris*. She made the New Bedford to Nantucket run, adding inter-island transportation between Martha's Vineyard and Nantucket. The passage from New Bedford to the Gray Lady took under seven hours and cost about two dollars.

Marco Bozzaris was followed in the 1830s by the 120-foot steamer *Telegraph*. She made three roundtrip passages each week between New Bedford and Nantucket, stopping at Vineyard Haven along the way. Owned by the Nantucket Steamboat Company, hers was a successful 25-year career. Joining her in the 1840s was the 160-foot long steamer *Massachusetts*. Both vessels made the runs from New Bedford, and beginning in 1854 from Hyannis, until their services were concluded just prior to the Civil War. Though the eventual fate of the *Telegraph* is unknown, the *Massachusetts* served during the war and then went on to almost 20 more years of service along the East Coast.

In the mid 1850s, the Nantucket Steamship Company became the Nantucket and Cape Cod Steamboat Company. During that time their newest vessel, *Island Home*, arrived at Hyannis. At a length of over 180 feet and nearly 500 tons, she was larger and deemed more reliable than previous vessels. *Island Home* serviced Nantucket for about 40 years. In 1902, after being converted to a barge, she was damaged by ice and lost off the coast of New Jersey.

Meanwhile, around the time that the *Island Home* was keeping Nantucket connected to the mainland, the vessel *Monohansett* was running between New Bedford and Martha's Vineyard. At about 175 feet in length and nearly 500 tons, she looked a lot like the *Island Home*. Owned by the New Bedford, Vineyard and Nantucket Steamboat Company, her relationship with the Vineyard lasted 40 years. *Monohansett* was sold off in 1903 and one year later she was wrecked in Salem Harbor.

Over a Half Century at Sea

In a town claiming hundreds of sea captains, it is a difficult task to choose one Dennis seafarer to represent the whole.

East Dennis had its Captain Crowells, Howes, Sears, and Halls. Dennisport had its Wixons and Kelleys. Dennis had more Howes, Halls, and Crowells, while South Dennis put forward its Thachers, Kelleys, Nickersons, and Bakers. And West Dennis, which produced the most sea captains, had its Studleys, Kelleys, Crowells, Bakers ... and Baxters.

Captain Joseph Baxter spent better than half a century at sea. In 1844, at age 10, he served as cook upon a vessel mastered by his father Obed Baxter. When he turned 19 he decided to go west, so he joined the crew of the clipper *Starlight* bound for San Francisco.

Over the next two years he sailed on a number of vessels along the California coast. Soon he was the master of his own ship, carrying freight between San Francisco and the other towns springing up along the west coast. Unfortunately, the gold rush economy went bust and in the end Baxter realized little profit from his hard work.

He became mate upon a vessel leaving San Francisco for the South Pacific in search of a cargo of fruit. For the good part of a year they hopped from island to island attempting to fill the ship's holds. At one such stop, the king of Guam wished for Baxter to marry his daughter, and by doing so to one day become king himself. The marriage never took place, and Baxter arrived back at San Francisco in 1856.

He immediately set sail for China on the clipper *Golden West*. After arriving at Hong Kong, he journeyed to Canton and became mixed up in a battle between the English and the Chinese. He later left China on board a ship headed for Cuba full of Chinese slaves. Though Baxter did not particularly like the idea of traveling on board a slave ship, he had no money and other options were not forthcoming.

With the Civil War raging, he was married in 1863, at age 29. The following year he sailed to Virginia in search of work. Instead he was drafted by the Navy and was made a pilot for the remainder of the war. His first assignment landed him on a gunboat headed up the Appomattox River, which was shot out from under him and sank. Afterward he was master of a number of vessels carrying ammunition, material, wounded Union soldiers, and Confederate prisoners of war.

At the war's end, Baxter returned to Dennis and teamed up with his brother Obed in the Atlantic coastal trade, shipping to ports throughout North and South America. For the next 17 years he sailed the Atlantic trade routes, returning home from time to time to be with his family.

In 1882, his wife passed away and so later that year he decided to set sail for the Pacific. For the remainder of his seafaring career, aboard the *Ralph M. Hayward*, he spent coasting that ocean's waters. He had a number of run-ins with Chinese pirates and South Sea island cannibals, but survived to return to West Dennis in 1899 where he retired from the sea after over a half century on her waves.

Captain Baxter earned his living upon the sea, as did hundreds of nineteenth century Cape Codders. Their journeys took them to faraway lands inhabited by exotic peoples. Yet this is the life they chose. Perhaps the salt of the ocean was in their blood, calling them from the rooted land to journey upon the rising and falling waves of the sea.

Sea Captains of the Ice Trade

Locally, on Cape Cod, ice became very important in the preservation of fish as consumers preferred "fresh," frozen fish over salted or smoked fish. Such street names as Freezer Road in Barnstable and Cold Storage Road in East Dennis attest to the efforts made to keep the fish catches fresh, and reveal a legacy of manufactured ice plants once located along the shore.

Cape Cod sea captains were also involved in the ice business, transporting cargoes of it all over the globe. The ice trade began in the early nineteenth century as vessels sailed for warmer lands to unload their mysterious cargo. In some lands the natives were afraid of ice as it "burned" their fingers. Others considered themselves swindled when the ice melted into nothing more than water! But the ice trade continued, even though upwards of 60% of the ice melted by the time the vessel reached its destination despite the speediest of passages and attempts at insulating the frigid cargo with sawdust.

In his first voyage as master, Captain Joshua Sears took his vessel *Burmah* and a cargo of ice from Boston to Calcutta in 1847. During that year, American ships transported over 22,000 tons of ice to foreign ports. Three years later, famed Orleans sea captain Ebenezer Linnell left Boston on board the vessel *Buena Vista* with a cargo of ice, bound for Calcutta. Linnell, known for his speed records, was annoyed at how the heavy cargo made for a sluggish passage.

Another sea captain who was not thrilled with his slow passage due to a cargo of ice was Captain John Taylor of Chatham. In 1878, as he sailed his vessel *Red Cloud* to Bombay, he wrote "The ship was all on her beam end and crank as all ice ships are, and of course could not carry any sail." One of the last shipments of ice to Barbados was accomplished by another Chatham man, Captain Levi D. Smith, aboard the bark *Florence* in 1880.

Falling Out of Love with the Sea

Cape Cod lads went to sea early, at age 15 or 16. They grew up before the mast, nearly all that they learned as they passed through the portal from boyhood to manhood they learned upon the ocean waves. By the time they were 20 they had been to the ports of Europe and Asia, and had traveled down one side of South America and up the other. As others headed west via covered wagon, they were heading west via Cape Horn. From the simple shores of Cape Cod they were journeying to see a world most Americans had never imagined.

When one considers Cape Cod sea captains, the name of Joshua Sears seems to appear near the top of the list. Perhaps it's because he led such a long and successful career upon the world's oceans, revered by all that knew him or sailed with him. Perhaps it's because of the ships he mastered, including the pride of the Shiverick clippers - the *Wild Hunter*, pushing each vessel to the absolute peak of her capabilities. Perhaps it's because he repre-sented the quintessential sea captain with his long white beard hiding a weathered face.

Or perhaps, given all of the above, it is because through his ship logs and letters he showed a human side not usually associated with a hardened and weathered sea captain. His writings tell of his deep inner thoughts, providing readers with a glimpse of life on the high seas.

At the age of 20 he was among the crew of the *Eben Preble*, commanded by Captain James Crocker, on a one-year voyage to China to pick up a cargo of tea. Within three years Sears rose to the rank of first mate of the *Preble*. Seven years later he became master of the *Burmah*. With his first command he established his reputa-tion as "a driver" by pushing his vessel and crew to produce speedy passages. During his years at sea he would out-race typhoons and pirates, and battle cholera and bouts of depression.

His next command was the *Orissa*, which he sailed a number of times to Calcutta during the 1850s, his wife Minerva and daughter Louise accompanying him on a number of his voyages. But his most perfect fit with a vessel would be his years as master of the magnificent clipper *Wild Hunter*. It was on this fine vessel that Captain Sears made his final voyage from 1857 to 1860 - a period of three and a half years! From Boston he made San Francisco four months later, then took the *Hunter* across the Pacific for Singapore - during the next three years acquiring cargoes where he could find them.

What follows are excerpts from Captain Sears' log. They give some indication of the inner thoughts of one of Cape Cod's foremost sea captains of the nineteenth century. They also speak of a captain who was falling out of love with the sea.

September 5, 1857: "That heavy swell keeps running from the west. Patience, patience – Put your trust in God."

September 6: "Slow getting going – Thy ways, O Lord, are inscrutable."

September 9: "The Lord is my Shepherd; He'll guide me safe through"

September 13: "O for a Cot in some Wilderness."

September 25: "Dead calm all this day; Current set the Ship 20 miles due East. I never had such hard luck before."

September 26: "Oh how disconsolate I do feel. Next voyage I will go down the China Sea and face all the Typhoons that blows."

By March of 1858 he was longing for home, far away from the China Sea. On March 10 he wrote: *"Oh for a home in some vast wilderness, where the waves of the ocean will trouble me no more."*

His state of homesickness had not improved a year later when, in April 1859, he wrote: *"Sometimes I feel as if I wanted to jump overboard, but now I have a great desire to live and see my home again."*

During the latter part of 1859 he fell ill, as reported in this letter home in December 1859: *"Four weeks ago ... I was taken with a sort of cholera so bad I thought I should hardly live through the night and I have not seen a well day since ... I think that I have got on the other side of the Hill and am sliding down, and when a person gets going, they are apt to go pretty fast ... I have never seen the need of a wife before so much as I have this voyage. But it will certainly take six months to get me tame enough to live with one ..."*

He goes on to write: *"Sometimes I get very homesick and think I cannot hardly stand it; and at other times it seems as if I did not care whether I ever see home again or not."*

Finally, in January 1860 he had secured cargo enough to head home. On July 19, off the coast of South America racing northward toward New York and the end of his seafaring career, Captain Sears wrote: *"If ever one poor fellow was tired of anything, it is I, Josh Sears, that is sick and tired of going to sea."*

When he arrived back on Cape Cod in autumn of 1860 he formerly retired. His sailing days ended, he spent his remaining 25 years with family and friends on dry land.

The Fastest Clipper Captain

Eastham's Freeman Hatch entered the nineteenth century maritime record books with an astonishing feat of seamanship. In 1852 he took his clipper ship *Northern Light* from San Francisco to Boston in the record time of 76 days and six hours.

It was a voyage that began on March 13 and pitted Hatch's new clipper against another new greyhound, the *Contest*, captained by William Brewster. The two ships raced evenly down the coast of Central America to the Line in 14 days. Captain Hatch aboard the *Northern Light* eventually gained a day on his rival and was at Cape Horn on the 38th day out.

Both ships made the eastward turn into the Atlantic in moderate breezes and snow squalls, still in sight of each other. The run north to Boston saw *Northern Light* arriving at Boston Light at 10 o'clock in the evening on May 28, 1852. She took another hour to glide to her pier. Captain Hatch had beaten *Contest* by two days and achieved the fastest passage of any sailing vessel between the two ports.

In 1993, Rich Wilson of Marblehead and Bill Biewenga of Newport, Rhode Island sailed their trimaran *Great American II* on the same route in 69 days and 20 hours, besting Captain Hatch by a full week. Purists would probably feel that the record-breaking effort of Wilson and Biewenga should carry an asterisk next to it as it was performed in a specially equipped vessel with navigational aids that were not available to Captain Hatch. Such critics would probably be the same as those who would not accept Roger Maris' 61 home run season because he played in eight more games than did Babe Ruth. At any rate, it is still impressive to stand in front of Captain Hatch's gravestone in Eastham and read:

Freeman Hatch, 1820-1889
He became famous making the astonishing passage in the
clipper ship Northern Light from San Francisco in 76 days
6 hours – an achievement won by no mortal before or since.

A Seafaring Cape Cod Town Without a Harbor

The town of Brewster has been credited by historians as having more sea captains in the 1800s than any other town of its size in America.

In Captain J. Henry Sears' book *Brewster Shipmasters*, published in 1906, he noted, "It is believed that more shipmasters engaged in foreign trade went from the town of Brewster than from any other town or place in the country in numerical proportion to its inhabitants. From a population numbering about one thousand people we have the names of one hundred and fifteen shipmasters living since the year 1840, and during the year 1850 there were over fifty living there at one time." Indeed, a book of vital statistics from the mid-1800s shows "mariner" as the most common occupation in the town.

One would certainly think that a town that was a nursery for so many shipmasters would have a harbor from which young men could become inspired to follow a life at sea. But Brewster has no harbor, nor does the town have any sort of river anchorage or even a protecting headland that might have been used as a storm refuge for ships.

Prior to 1840, ship traffic that originated from Brewster took its chances running the shallow channel at Paines' Creek at high tide, or sloops and small schooners skirted bluffs at Point of Rocks to anchor near the bay shore, settling awkwardly onto the sand flats at low tide. In 1733, a proposal to erect a stone pier at Point of Rocks was voted down. There was also a proposal in 1806 to dam up Paine's Creek to create an artificial harbor, but it was never accomplished.

In the 1840s, the seagoing needs of Brewster were finally improved with the building of a stone breakwater to the east of Sears Point and north of the center of town. The breakwater was connected to the shore by a wooden wharf. A "T" shaped pier was

built on the breakwater itself with a depression dug on the lee side
to allow vessels to settle safely upright when the tide receded. A
number of 60 to 80-ton packets called at the breakwater including
the schooners, *Patriot, Sarah,* and *Chatham.* During the 1850s, the
steamer *Naushon* connected passengers to Plymouth and Boston
from the site.

The arrival of the railroad into Brewster at the end of the Civil War
put an end to regular packet traffic to the town. The breakwater and
its wharf fell into disrepair. By the beginning of the twentieth
century there was little to mark the location of Brewster's artificial
harbor. Today a person can stand on the bluff above the sand flats at
the end of Breakwater Beach Road and still see the remains of the
ballast stones that were part of the pier structure. Nothing further
remains to mark the place where many of the young men of Cape
Cod's "Sea Captain Town" began their illustrious careers.

A Speedy and Skillful Master

At 251-feet in length and 2,300 tons, the beautiful clipper *Red
Jacket* was built for speed. Launched in 1853, she left New York
Harbor on January 11, 1854 with Captain Asa Eldridge of
Yarmouth as her master.

Red Jacket made the crossing to Liverpool's Mersey River in
record time - 13 days, one hour and 25 minutes - a sailing ship
record that still stands to this day! On one day alone, *Red Jacket*
traveled an amazing 413 miles. Nearly every day of the journey the
ship encountered stormy weather. Upon her arrival at Liverpool,
the speedy *Red Jacket* was sold to the British for a tidy profit.

Her master, Captain Eldridge, was one of three seafaring brothers. All three started in the Liverpool packet service. In fact,
brother John was master of the appropriately named vessel
Liverpool on which the third brother, Oliver, was mate. Meanwhile,
Asa took command of the *Roscious* and earned such a name for
himself as a speedy and skillful master that he was first choice for
master when the *Red Jacket* was launched. Kittredge, in his book
Cape Cod: It's People and Their History refers to Eldridge as "the
most distinguished shipmaster that the Cape ever produced" and

"among the world's half dozen greatest shipmasters."

After his *Red Jacket* fame, Eldridge was appointed master of the equally famous Collins Line steamer *Pacific*. Previously, in May 1851, Captain Ezra Nye of Sandwich raced the 2,700-ton, 280-foot long *Pacific* across the Atlantic from New York to Liverpool in nine days, 20 hours and 16 minutes, setting a new record.

So, with the marriage of the speedy *Pacific* and her equally speedy new master, all indications seemed to point to many more record passages. Shortly after Eldridge took command, though, the *Pacific* was lost in 1856 upon Atlantic waters. Though there were no survivors to validate the claim, some believe that the boilers blew as the storied Yarmouth sea captain pushed his new command to the limit, reaching for yet another speed record. Historians may never know what happened for sure, as the sea holds well her many secrets.

The Last Coasterman

Cape Cod is full of stories about sailors who made a name for themselves at sea. Some of these men saw the ocean as a source of making a living while others took to it for the adventure that it provided. For the better part of three centuries, Cape Codders made seafaring a part of their personal resumes because it was a natural part of living near the ocean.

It is doubtful that anyone could say who was the first "Blue Water Man" from Cape Cod. These men sailed the larger vessels across the great oceans of the world. There were literally hundreds of them. Some went on to international fame and financial success. Many became community leaders when they left the business of the sea, chartering banks, pursuing political office, and running the ubiquitous village dry goods stores. A good many of these legendary captains got their start as "coastermen," hauling the nation's granite, lumber, coal, and ice into ports like Stonington, Darien, Wilmington, and Jacksonville. They were skilled in navigating tidal channels and dangerous shoal waters.

Coasting captains sailed their small 50- to 60-ton schooners until the railroads drove them out of business at the end of the last

century. Of the few coastermen who remained in the trade, most
continued to follow the familiar patterns of hauling coal from
northern ports to destinations in the Carolinas and southward
along the East Coast. They returned to New England with lumber
or perhaps with fruit obtained via a side trip to the Bahamas.

One Cape Cod shipmaster that continued in the coasting business until well into the twentieth century was Captain Bennett D.
Coleman of Cotuit. While it is never safe to claim title to be the first
or last of anything, a strong case can be made that Captain
Coleman was the last coasting captain from Cape Cod to work
exclusively under sail.

Captain Coleman was born in Cotuit on October 27, 1868. He
came from a family of seafaring men and by the age of 13 was
aboard ship as a cook. He took his first command at the age of 20
aboard the three-masted schooner *Thomas B. Garland*. For a number
of years he commanded coasting schooners owned by Commodore
Edwin P. Bogs of Falmouth.

On two occasions he experienced disasters at sea, once in a
winter storm off Delaware and another time when his ship, the
George D. Edmands, caught fire two nights out of Bermuda while on
a trip to Nova Scotia. In that event, Captain Coleman and his crew
spent eight days and nights in an open boat before being rescued.

Shortly after the First World War, when he was in his fifties,
Captain Coleman joined a partnership that purchased the four-
masted schooner *Anna R. Heidritter* and he became the vessel's
master. The *Heidritter* was a solidly built craft constructed at Bath,
Maine in 1903. She was 185 feet in length and displaced almost 700
tons. Through the 1920s and 1930s Captain Coleman took the
vessel on voyages between New England and the Caribbean, as
well as to a number of southern ports. Home ported in New York
City, the *Heidritter* was a familiar visitor to such ports as Providence, New Bedford, and harbors along the Connecticut coast.

Occasionally the captain brought the ship into Boston with a
load of lumber. A family reunion would be held at the East Boston
Piers where the ship tied up. From Boston to St. Augustine,
lighthouse keepers and harbor pilots kept a special lookout for the
Heidritter and her captain. She was virtually the last of the once

great fleet of coastal windjammers that had crowded the shipping lanes in earlier days.

At the end of the 1930s, when he was nearing 70 years of age, Captain Coleman was making regular voyages to the West Indies, traveling out with coal and returning with logwood or fertilizer. In December of 1940, he sailed the *Heidritter* from Newport News, Virginia with a cargo of coal for Guadeloupe. From this island he sailed to Las Piedras in Venezuela. The ship had a hard voyage and limped into Charleston, South Carolina on March 13, 1941, her sails in rags.

Captain Coleman left the ship in Charleston to undergo a serious operation. It was supposed to be just a temporary "grounding" for the man who had spent a lifetime as sea. He had retired several times earlier in his career, but he never seemed contented with life ashore. While Coleman was recovering in Charleston, the *Heidritter* made several more trips to the West Indies with another master in charge. In February of 1942, as the vessel was en route from Haiti to Chester, Pennsylvania, the new captain took sick and the *Heidritter* put into Charleston. Captain Coleman resumed command with the intention of completing the trip.

After running for the Delaware River for several days, Captain Coleman marked his position south of Cape Hatteras. The United States was now a participant in World War II and German submarines were a constant threat to ships passing along the Atlantic coast. The *Heidritter* was sailing much closer to the shore because of this danger. Rather than attempting to pass Cape Hatteras at night without visual navigation aids, Captain Coleman anchored the *Heidritter* in 13 fathoms of water off Ocracoke Island. His intention was to make a run north around Cape Hatteras at first light. But while the ship was at anchor, the wind shifted and the *Heidritter* began to drag her anchors. Despite all efforts, the crew was unable to hold the ship in position and she struck the bar stern first in the early morning hours of March 3, 1942. The vessel became a total loss.

At 73 years of age, Captain Coleman had survived with his life but not with his ship. While he acknowledged his good fortune at being alive, there was resignation in his appraisal of his vessel's sad end. "We were lucky to get out," he recalled. "If the masts had gone on the shoals, we would have gone with them. But she was a strong old craft. Has weathered many gales with me and died honestly. I did not run her ashore. We tried our best for two hours to keep her off."

In the next week, Captain Coleman was able to get out to the wreck only once due to bad weather. He described his visit to the hulk like "going to a funeral." The old sailor was able to salvage his sextants and the chronometer from the flooded cabin. He wrote to his family that his prospects didn't seem good. He mentioned the possibility of another ship, but seemed resigned to the fact that it might be "time to give it a trial ashore - may find something to do around those boatyards at Falmouth."

But despite any plans that he might have had, Captain Coleman did not long survive the death of his ship. He was killed less than two weeks after the wreck in an automobile crash in Newark, New Jersey as he traveled home to Cape Cod. The hazards of travel on land curiously proved more deadly than that which the sea had supplied him for over half a century.

Chapter 6

Shipwrecks & Lighthouses

No landsman can appreciate the power of the ocean until he is actually transported to the heart of its stormy domain.

Cape Codders took to the sea out of necessity as a means of connecting with the world beyond the peninsula. Local inhabitants knew that the ocean held the key to success and failure, indeed, life and death, and they always regarded Neptune's backyard with awe and respect. Standing on the sandy bluffs of the outer Cape in Wellfleet and Truro, watching a winter storm smash foaming waves against the vulnerable beach, it is possible to get a sense of where this deference for one of Mother Nature's most powerful forces came from.

From the very first shipwreck in 1626 when the small English sloop *Sparrowhawk* went ashore on Nauset Beach, thousands of vessels have ended their days on what many have termed "the sailors graveyard" – Cape Cod. Despite the efforts of the Life Saving Service, which was established in the late nineteenth century, and the presence of a number of lighthouses strategically placed along the coastline, many mariners nevertheless fell victim to the dangerous shoals, unfavorable winds, and tidal currents that marked the passage around Cape Cod. Some sailors were in sight of their final destination after having sailed thousands of miles when their vessels foundered off the Cape, leaving their bones to rest for eternity in lonely Cape Cod burial grounds.

Lost At Sea!

An epitaph from a Truro gravestone:
*"The Lord said I will bring my people
again from the depths of the sea."*

In the middle of the last century when Henry David Thoreau visited the town of Truro, he made an inquiry about one of the houses in the town. "Who lives there?" he asked. "Three widows," was the reply. Each of the women had lost their seafaring husband to the treacherous sea.

Thoreau was wise enough to see that there was good reason for Cape Codders to dislike the ever-present sound of the pounding surf. And while he was not a resident of the seacoast himself, he soon learned from many conversations with the local inhabitants that the sea could be a cruel and merciless neighbor. As he stood on the great Atlantic beach, Thoreau reflected on how much suffering the sea had caused there. "The ancients would have represented it as a sea-monster with open jaws," he wrote. "More terrible than Scylla and Charybdis."

A walk through almost any Cape Cod cemetery will reveal the enormous cost in young lives that was historically associated with living in a sea front community. This was something of which Cape Codders were always conscious.

There was even an old saying that "Death occurs at ebb tide." While today we live in an age that increasingly seems to consume its young men in often senseless acts of human violence, earlier centuries saw Cape families losing their fathers, uncles, brothers, and sons to the natural forces of storm and surf. The gravestones of those lost at sea serve to mark the memories of people who did not return to those who waited anxiously at home. Their deaths

had great impact in the small Cape villages. In October of 1841, for
example, 57 men from Truro were lost in a gale. At that time, Truro
had less than one thousand inhabitants. In that same storm, Dennis
lost 28 sailors. The stones that express such losses seem to be
designed to send a message to the viewer through the poetry that
is carved beneath the names.

> *"They sleep beneath the blue lone sea*
> *They lie where pearls lie deep,*
> *They were the loved of all.*
> *Yet not o'er their low beds may we weep."*

Another epitaph is equally poignant:

> *"My body on the wreck was found*
> *and now lies buried under ground*
> *From the raging sea my spirit did fly,*
> *to reign with God above the sky"*

"In memory of Warren Freeman who died at sea ..." (J. Coogan photo)

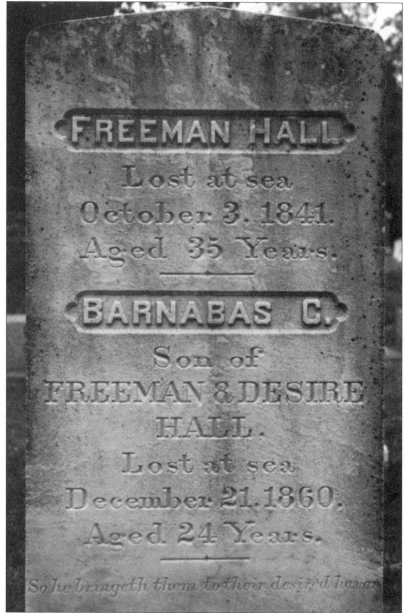

Father and son lost at sea two decades apart – Freeman Hall during the great gale of October 1841 and Barnabas C. Hall lost in 1860. (A. Sheedy photo)

Often the circumstances that surrounded death at sea lay shrouded in the depths of the ocean. "Drowned at Wilmington," "Lost off the Ocracoke," or "Lost on his passage to Mediera," are inscriptions that provide few details of a seaman's final moments. In other cases, the record is very clear and visible on the stone.

The old North Truro burying ground gives us the story of Daniel Cassity, whose marker notes that he lost his life in early 1852 while attempting to rescue surviving crewmembers of the stranded British ship *Josephus*. Observers saw Cassity and another Truro man, Jonathan Collins, attempt to launch a boat into the surf only to be swept to their deaths in the breakers. Cassity was 23 years old. His gravestone includes the names of two other members of the Cassity family who were also lost at sea. Andrew Cassity was drowned in 1816 at the age of 16 and brother Timothy was lost in the Bay of Chaleur at the Gaspe Peninsula at age eighteen.

Occasionally the poetry on the gravestone can give a gripping image of the doomed sailor's final moments. In the Harwich Center burying ground next to the Congregational Church there is a stone that remembers 23-year-old Cyrus Blanchard and his death at sea off Provincetown in 1841:

"Once on the raging seas I rode.
The storm was loud, the night was dark.
The ocean yawn'd and rudely blow'd
the wind that tossed my foundring bark.
Deep horror then my vitals frose:
Death struck: I ceas'd the tide to slow."

"A mysterious, inexplicable affair"

Cape Cod has had its share of mysteries over its nearly four centuries since settlement. The foggy tale of the *Abigail* is one such tale so clouded in mystery that even today it makes as little sense as it did in 1772.

It is a tale that was so talked about in its day that colonial Governor Thomas Hutchinson was among those who presided over the eventual court case. Boston lawyer and future US President John Adams defended the accused. It would not be Adams's first controversial court case, as he had earlier defended the British troops who fired on an angry mob in 1770, killing five townspeople in what would become known as the Boston Massacre.

This latest case involved a Chatham man by the name of Ansel Nickerson, the sole survivor of an apparent massacre on board the schooner *Abigail*, just off the coast of Cape Cod. The vessel was discovered by a Captain Joseph Doane Jr. on November 15, 1772 adrift off the coast of Chatham, a signal of distress fluttering above her. Doane boarded the vessel to find only one man on the ship and evidence of some damage in the form of a barrel of rum broken open. Nickerson, the sole crewmember, was found in a state of distress and was described by Doane as being quite frightened.

The survivor told a tale that began with the *Abigail* leaving Boston Harbor for a short journey across Massachusetts Bay and down the backside of the Cape to Chatham, and concluded with claims of piracy, plunder, kidnap, and murder. On board the vessel with Ansel Nickerson were his two cousins, Thomas Nickerson and Sparrow Nickerson, their brother-in-law Elisha Newcomb, and a 13-year old boy named William Kent, Jr. In the early morning hours of that November day, according to Ansel's testimony, a British schooner emerged from the darkness and came alongside the *Abigail*. Afraid that he would be "impressed" to serve aboard the British vessel, Ansel went over the side of the ship, hanging from a rope out of sight.

According to Ansel Nickerson, these British pirates murdered the two Nickerson men and Newcomb, stole some of the ship's cargo – including rum – and kidnapped the young Kent boy. After they left, Ansel climbed back on board to witness the carnage. He then remained on board in a stupor until the drifting *Abigail* was discovered by Captain Doane. The vessel was towed to port and Doane reported the events to the authorities in Barnstable. Nickerson's story, though, did not make sense to those who considered the strange case of the *Abigail*, so he was subsequently arrested and taken away to Boston for trial. While this was being done, a search for a pirate vessel of Nickerson's description was conducted, but no such vessel was found. All eyes shifted to the Chatham man as the perpetrator of the terrible murders.

Even before John Adams was named to defend Nickerson, he was already thinking and writing in his journal about these bizarre events off Cape Cod. He described it in his journal as "a mysterious, inexplicable affair." One must believe that Adams raised his eyebrows a bit when he first learned of the events surrounding the case, for the plundered vessel shared the name of his own wife – Abigail.

Ansel Nickerson's story became more and more unbelievable. Captain Doane's testimony did not include the bloody decks that Nickerson had described. Was the Admiralty Court to believe that three men could be butchered without a drop of blood? And what of the bodies? If they were tossed overboard in the vicinity of Chatham shouldn't they have washed up on a Cape beach? Even the damage to the ship as told by Nickerson could neither be verified nor corroborated by Captain Doane. The only piece of evidence that Doane would corroborate was that a barrel of rum, as Nickerson had stated, was broken into and was left at low tide with only a few gallons of the liquor remaining. Other than that, all else was "normal" according to Captain Doane's testimony.

And yet, if Nickerson was guilty of murder, how could one man have overpowered three men to take command of the ship? What would have been the motive for such actions? Regardless, Nickerson was formally charged with murder and piracy, to which he pleaded innocent. A trial was scheduled for July 1773.

A five-day trial ensued, during which the prosecution could not prove beyond a reasonable doubt that Nickerson had performed the accused deeds. Adams's defense of Nickerson maintained that the Chatham man was a lucky survivor of a pirate attack on the high seas, and that he was not in any way involved in the murders, nor the pillage of the ship's cargo. After two hours of deliberation, the judges returned with a four-to-four split vote, and therefore a "not guilty" verdict for the defendant. He was cleared of all charges and set free. Despite the acquittal, the people of Boston, Cape Cod, and the rest of Massachusetts could not be certain of what had happened aboard the *Abigail* during that November night.

Even Adams was left confused by the whole *Abigail* ordeal. After the trial he penned in his diary, "This was and remains still a mysterious transaction. I know not to this day what judgement to form of his guilt or innocence." He went on to write many years after the trial, "I suppose the want of direct evidence afforded room for doubt in the minds of the majority."

Conflicting accounts and twisted evidence continued to envelop the case in a shroud of confusion. Some retellings of the story state that Captain Doane witnessed the bloodstained decks of the *Abigail* and even saw the bodies of the two Nickerson men and Newcomb on the vessel, their chests ripped open as evidence of the carnage. This last bit of testimony may be some confusion over the word "chest" for Doane could also have been referring to sea chests, as in lockers, ripped open rather than the victims' chests.

Other accounts clearly state that Doane witnessed no bodies and no blood at all. Some accounts point to a British ship while other accounts suggest a band of French pirates. It has been suggested that Ansel Nickerson was put on trial two times, and each time he was found not guilty. At least one source spells Nickerson's name as "Anson," while another source reveals that Ansel was not really his name at all, but rather Levi.

It is interesting to note that he was married exactly one year to the day before the *Abigail* affair, on November 14, 1771, to a Mary Smith of Chatham. His life after the *Abigail* affair remains rather murky. Most accounts show that Nickerson went on to live another decade and a half. It is believed he fought for the cause of independence against the crown during the Revolutionary War.

His death in the West Indies is also a source of controversy. One story has him convicted of murder on the island of Saint Eustatius, in the Netherlands Antilles, where he was put to death by hanging. Another tale states that as Nickerson lay dying on the island of Martinique he confessed to the murders on board the *Abigail*. Yet, the validity of that confession remains as cloudy as the rest of the events surrounding one of the Cape's most bizarre and most guarded mysteries.

Yarmouth Lighthouses at "Peak" Performance

During the nineteenth century, and even into the first decades of the twentieth century, the beams of at least one lighthouse shone over Yarmouth's southern shoreline for a period of 112 years.

The first lighthouse, known as Point Gammon, was built at the southwestern tip of Great Island in 1816, at the entrance to Hyannis Harbor. Consisting of some 600 acres, Great Island was first settled in the 1640s by Yelverton Crowe. Set off as it was from the rest of the town of Yarmouth, the island was home to a smallpox hospital during the early years of the nineteenth century. It was also home to saltworks and lamp black production.

The original keeper of the lighthouse was Samuel Peak who held the post until his death in the mid-1820s. His son John took over the duties for the next 30 years, until the lighthouse was eventually discontinued in 1858. John Peak then made the move to the recently completed Bishop and Clerks lighthouse constructed some three miles south of Point Gammon, out upon the waters of Nantucket Sound where a series of boulders had menaced mariners for decades. These rocks had at one time been part of a five-acre island that disappeared under the waves of the sound in the mid-1700s. A lightship marked the dangerous underwater boulders until the lighthouse could be built.

Like Point Gammon light, Bishop and Clerks lighthouse stood 70 feet tall. It also housed a fog bell. This lighthouse remained in service until 1928. The Point Gammon site was dismantled in 1935 after many years of decay and neglect. Bishops and Clerks remained "on guard" in the sound until 1952, although its light had been silenced for a quarter century. It was finally dynamited, a beacon now marking the spot.

For more than half a century the lighthouses of Yarmouth were operated at "peak" performance by the father and son team of Samuel and John Peak. Their decades of service, day after day, night after night, is representative of the many men and woman who, over the centuries, kept the lights burning to warn mariners of the dangers along the tricky Cape coastline.

A Sea Captain's Premonition?

It is said that Abraham Lincoln had a dream just before his death that foretold of his impending doom. Was his dream a window to the future, or just Lincoln's subconscious mind admitting that, with the Civil War coming to a close and strong southern hatred for him boiling over, an assassination attempt was not beyond possibility?

A little known author by the name of Morgan Robertson penned a novel in 1898 about a huge, unsinkable ocean liner some 800 feet long that hits an iceberg in the middle of the Atlantic Ocean on an April evening without enough lifeboats for everyone on board. The author named the fictitious vessel *Titan*. Was Robertson's novel a premonition of the *Titanic* disaster to occur 14 years later, or just a strange coincidence?

Perhaps some of the most superstitious people were those who sailed upon the sea. The stories abound of ships and sea captains that were considered cursed as if Poseidon himself held a personal grudge. A number of Cape sea captains wrecked two or even three vessels over the course of their seafaring career … and were eventually told to look inland for future employment opportunities. Were these shipmasters cursed souls or just bad mariners? Most likely it was a combination of both.

One very well respected Cape Cod sea captain was Centerville's Josiah Richardson. Over the course of a 32-year career he rose up through the ranks to become one of the country's premier shipmasters and in May 1852 was rewarded with the command of the new clipper *Staffordshire*. At 240 feet in length, and well appointed to accommodate oceangoing passengers in the greatest level of comfort and luxury available, she was perhaps the greatest vessel afloat in her day. Her lines were beautiful with artistic woodwork decorating her stern, depicting an English scene on one side and an American scene on the other.

Yet doom awaited the *Staffordshire* between these two sides of the Atlantic.

Bad omens seemed to haunt the ship right from the beginning, stemming from the fact that the *Staffordshire* carried a figurehead in the form of a white witch. Two sisters, Margaret and Catherine Fox, who were mediums from Arcadia, New York, announced that the figurehead would cause disaster for the vessel, her crew, and her passengers. The sisters, who had helped to bring about the

American spiritual movement in 1848 when they reported hearing rapping noises in their home, had a large and devoted legion of followers – about one million strong by the mid-1850s. In fact, so widespread became these latest predictions of doom for the *Staffordshire* that the ship's departure from Boston was delayed. Eventually she was on her way, on May 3, 1852, and arrived safely at San Francisco after a 101-day voyage, breaking a number of speed records along the way.

Richardson then took his new command across the Pacific to India, breaking more records including a speedy 83-day passage home from Calcutta to Boston. It is suggested that Richardson could have made the journey even one day shorter had he braved some nasty weather as he approached the New England coast. Though his calculation of position proved to be correct after all, he took the safer option and reduced speed in order to avoid trouble. Richardson was a sea captain for all seasons, speedy yet cautious and always accommodating.

Later in 1853, Richardson sailed the *Staffordshire* across the Atlantic to Liverpool. His letters home to his wife during November and December of that year suggest a man with his finger on the pulse of future events. In occasional dark reflections, the usually steady and skilled shipmaster seems to have possessed misgivings about the upcoming journey home. His letters were filled with premonitions of disaster as represented by the following:

November 11: "Should much prefer selling the ship and returning home in steamer … many accidents have occurred to the best ships and the most able commanders."

November 18: "Wish I was with you and did not have to make the western passage."

December 5: "In case of any accident to me, this will show how my account stands with (the Staffordshire's owners) … Life is uncertain, we both know, and all the property I possess I wish my dear wife and children to have and enjoy."

Staffordshire left Liverpool with nearly 200 passengers and crew, and "the greatest amount of freight on board ever taken from Liverpool to Boston" according to Captain Richardson. About two weeks at sea, on December 23, a terrific storm did damage to the ship, twisting the rudder-head. More damage during a gale on December 28 took away "the bowsprit, foretopmast, fore yard and everything forward" according to first mate Joseph Alden. Later that day Richardson, who went aloft to examine the damage, fell some 35 feet to the deck below, severely damaging his back. He was taken to his cabin where he was attended by the ship's surgeon and made as comfortable as possible. From his cot Richardson gave orders, but conditions continued to worsen.

The ship's crew, working under the direction of First Mate Alden, attempted to make repairs to the latest damage inflicted on the vessel. But another storm hit the ship on December 29, turning into "a hurricane" according to Alden. Just around midnight the *Staffordshire* struck rocks near Sable Island, south of Nova Scotia. The ship drifted away from the rocks, her hull breached, and began to settle as water flooded inside the mighty vessel. At first Alden considered beaching her, but with limited maneuverability and a crew in disorder, the thought was quickly dashed. Pumps were employed, but 14 inches of water in the hold quickly grew to four feet over the course of 10 minutes. It was clear that the ship would not survive, so efforts began toward saving the passengers and crew.

Richardson, still in his cot, realized that his feelings of dread had come true. He had one last hope ... he figured the water was shallow enough that the vessel's hull would hit bottom before she submerged completely. Alden, though, informed him that the ship had drifted into deeper waters and would sink. According to his testimony, the first mate offered to carry his captain to a lifeboat. Richardson declined the offer, reportedly saying, "Then I am lost, God's will be done." and down he went with his vessel. Some 175 people were lost in what became one of the most tragic passenger wrecks of the nineteenth century.

Those who believe in such things will say that the *Staffordshire* was indeed cursed, for she tempted Fate by carrying a figurehead in the form of a white witch and because of that she met doom at midnight, the witching hour. No doubt, in Arcadia, New York, the Fox sisters were heard to say, "We told you so!"

When Family Ties Kept a Lighthouse Bright

Bass River was an important mid-Cape shipping center in the nineteenth century. In addition to the busy river traffic that visited South Yarmouth village, the area of Nantucket Sound off West Dennis was a place where ships bound around Monomoy shoals would anchor and wait for fair winds and tides before attempting the run around that dangerous promontory. Because of the large volume of ship traffic, a lighthouse was established on the eastern side of the river mouth in the spring of 1855.

But in 1880, the U.S. government failed to renew funds for the operation of the Bass River lighthouse. Captain William Garfield of West Dennis decided to take the problem directly to the highest official in the land, the President of the United States!

Captain Garfield was the master of the schooner *O. D. Witherall* and a respected member of the community of master mariners then residing in West Dennis. Not a native Cape Codder, Garfield had been born in Ohio. He moved to Cape Cod as a teenager and worked his way up in the seafaring trade, eventually commanding his own vessel. His Ohio lineage included the newly elected President James Garfield, and the captain used his family connection to personally lobby for the continued operation of the Bass River Light.

Shortly after President Garfield's election, Captain Garfield wrote a letter to his relative about the situation at Bass River.

"I drop you a line or two again on account of a Light House we have here that has been standing for twenty five years and last October was put out by the Lighthouse Board. We have sent in a large partition (sic) for them to relight it again. Our Harbor is one of the best that there is in the Vineyard Sound. All vessels come in here in bad weather and no light makes it bad for large vessels. When you git (sic) to Washington and git (sic) everything working, well then, we shall write you and see if you can do anything for this Light House."

At the end of June of 1881, Captain Garfield went to Washington D.C. for a visit with the President. On the evening of July 1, the captain and his two daughters were invited to the White House for dinner. At around 8 o'clock in the evening, as the men enjoyed an after dinner cigar, the President turned to the captain and told him that as of that moment, by executive order, the Bass River Light was being re-lit. Somehow, with presidential prodding, the Lighthouse Board had found the funds for the continued operation of the beacon.

The Bass River Light subsequently continued to light the way for mariners until 1914 when it was finally disestablished. Ironically, the presidential order to keep the light operating was one of the last official acts accomplished by President Garfield. On July 2, 1881, before Captain Garfield had risen to check out of his hotel to begin his journey back to Cape Cod, the President was shot by an assassin, the wound eventually proving fatal some two and a half months later.

Women of the Lights

Since the early eighteenth century, lighthouses have guided mariners around the dangerous shoal waters of Cape Cod and the Islands. For the most part, the lighthouse keepers were men, often retired seafarers who knew the value of a navigation beacon on a stormy night. But there were a few women who became full-time keepers in the nineteenth century and it does not seem that the safety of sailors at sea was in any way compromised by their unusual occupation.

Perhaps the earliest female lighthouse keeper on Cape Cod was Angeline Nickerson, who succeeded her husband Simeon Nickerson as full-time keeper of the Chatham twin lights from 1848 to 1859. Apparently, there was some initial grumbling by some of the citizens of the town and there was a movement to have her replaced by a man. But Mrs. Nickerson had her supporters and a number of them came to her defense. Resident Joshua Nickerson (undoubtedly a cousin) went so far as to write a letter to President Zachary Taylor in which he stated that, "she had discharged her duties ... in a most careful and faithful manner." The campaign to bring in a new keeper at Chatham soon stopped.

Sandy Neck Light, which was situated at the bayside entrance to Barnstable Harbor, had two female lighthouse keepers. Lucy J.

Baxter was in charge of this light between 1862 and 1867, succeeding her husband F. T. Baxter. This was a period when the harbor was very active with vessels arriving from and traveling to all parts of the world. Records indicate that Eunice Crowell Howes, wife of Jacob Stone Howes, also ran the lighthouse for two years in the late part of the nineteenth century.

Another Cape woman, Sarah Cleverly Atwood of Wellfleet was appointed as keeper of the Mayo Beach Light in Wellfleet Harbor in 1876. She was the widow of William N. Atwood, a disabled Civil War veteran who had held the job since his return from the war. At his death it seems that the most qualified person to carry on the duties of the light was his wife. She assisted him for years to the point that she knew everything there was to know about the operation of the beacon.

Realizing that they had the perfect candidate for the job already living there, the government, in a rare demonstration of logic, turned the responsibilities over to Mrs. Atwood. She remained as keeper until 1891 when she resigned and moved "uptown" to East

The old Bass River Light, built in 1855 and still in operation today. (A. Sheedy photo)

Commercial Street. "Aunt Sarah," as she was known to scores of Wellfleet youngsters, continued to be a fixture in the town until her death at the age of 83 on November 20, 1920.

The Strange Loss of the Carrie D. Knowles

Many ships sailed from Cape Cod and never returned. One of the strangest tales of a vessel lost at sea was the story of the Provincetown whaler *Carrie D. Knowles*. In January of 1904, the schooner left the Cape tip under the command of Captain Collin Stevenson.

The ship had been a mainstay of the Provincetown whaling fleet since her first voyage in 1887. Owned by George Osborn Knowles of Provincetown, and built in Essex, Massachusetts, by the end of 1903 the *Carrie D. Knowles* had made 16 successful whaling voyages. This time she was bound initially for St. Vincent in the British West Indies before venturing out into the Atlantic whaling grounds.

The passage from Cape Cod to the West Indies normally took about three weeks, but after over two months there was no word as to the ship's arrival there. More months went by and the sad reality that the ship must have foundered with all hands brought a pall of sadness to the Cape tip. Five years passed and the survivors of the lost crew went about re-establishing their lives.

But in the spring of 1909 a letter arrived from Kingstown in the West Indies announcing that Captain Stevenson and his crew were being held in a Venezuelan prison! The story came out on the word of a sailor who had Cape Cod roots and who claimed to have escaped from the same prison. The sailor, whose name was Elisha Payne, claimed that he saw the crew of the *Knowles* arrive from their damaged vessel and that they were being secretly held in a damp and confining prison. He alone claimed to have escaped with great difficulty from the prison and made his way to St. Vincent. Apparently they were being held by the Venezuelan government for ransom. Relations between the United States and Venezuela were not good at that time and the tale was believed by many people who felt that this was something that might well have happened to Americans in an unfriendly South American country. Payne, the source of this information, however soon disappeared so authorities had no chance to further question him about the veracity of his story.

In Provincetown there was naturally great consternation. Insurance claims on the vessel had recently been paid. Several crewmembers' wives had already taken new husbands. The wife of Captain Stevenson had made plans to remarry. Word of the possible imprisonment of her husband caused her to cancel the wedding.

The character of Payne as a source of truth came into question from several quarters. He was characterized as a person of some ill repute by people who knew him in New Bedford. In Truro, a newspaper correspondent who remembered him living there under the name Paine did not give him a ringing endorsement. When the U.S. government tried to get more information about the situation in Venezuela, there was nothing to support Payne's allegations.

Still, what Payne told authorities in St. Vincent seemed to be information that only a true witness could have known. There was no apparent motive to indicate that he had anything to gain by crafting such a cruel hoax. The doubts lingered long after the prison tale and many were convinced that there was substance to the story. Certainly a number of residents of the Cape tip believed that somewhere in Venezuela some of their townsmen were suffering a terrible fate.

Yet even after years of speculation and false hope nothing ever came of efforts to get more information about what happened to the *Carrie D. Knowles* and her crew. It remains one of Cape Cod's strangest tales of a ship lost at sea.

Wreck of the Charlotte T. Sibley

Yarmouth is not known for a coastline that has attracted many shipwrecks over the centuries, not like the communities along the outer arm of the Cape with bars and shoals that have witnessed some 3,000 wrecks over the past 400 years.

Yet, on October 7, 1907 the turbulent seas of Nantucket Sound, off South Yarmouth, must have seemed like the dangerous waters off Provincetown's Peaked Hill Bars for the captain and crew of the *Charlotte T. Sibley*. A three-masted schooner, the *Sibley* was anchored about a mile offshore in an attempt to outlast a storm packing near hurricane force winds of 70 miles per hour. Captain Hatch of the *Sibley* and his crew of six had enlisted the services of four anchor lines to keep the vessel from being tossed about. As the force of the storm heightened, the port anchor chain parted, followed by a second, sending the *Sibley* violently lurching with the pounding waves.

About a half mile from shore the vessel became grounded on the bars and the seas engulfed her. As the decks became awash with waves, the captain ordered his crew into the rigging in a desperate attempt to save their lives. Without a rescue attempt they were doomed, yet the nearest lifesaving station was across the water at Monomoy, an impossible 15 miles away. But a rescue effort did commence, out of Bass River in the form of the 40-foot powerboat *Ildico*, commanded by Captain Charles Henry Davis with a crew of four volunteers.

Once the *Ildico* cleared the safety of the jetties that marked the entrance to Bass River, the rest of the journey out to the stricken *Charlotte T. Sibley* was a battle. By the time the rescue boat arrived at the wreck, Captain Hatch and his crew had abandoned their vessel in a small boat. After a number of attempts, the *Sibley* crew retrieved a line from the *Ildico* and the shipwrecked mariners were taken ashore, all lives saved.

Later, Captain Hatch, in praise of his rescuers, said, "Massachusetts breeds men and no Cape Cod man ever stood by and watched a man drown if there was a chance - only one chance in a thousand – of saving him."

Cape Cod's Titanic Connection

Best estimates suggest that this peninsula has produced 3,000 shipwrecks over the centuries. Many of these vessels had nothing at all to do with Cape Cod, merely passing along her shore en route to Boston or New York or some other port.

For instance, the *Portland*, which sank north of Race Point on

November 27, 1898, was actually trying to make her way from Boston to Portland, Maine, yet she was beaten and battered by a terrible storm across Massachusetts Bay to founder in Cape waters. The outer shore of Cape Cod was merely the recipient of her wreckage and her dead, and these waters became her tomb for the past 100 years.

Other shipwrecks had even less to do with Cape Cod except for a few thin strands of thread that somehow, though delicately, form a connection between the two. Such is the case with the greatest shipwreck of them all – *RMS Titanic*.

Although the sinking of the *Titanic* occurred over 1,200 miles away from our most outermost shores, out in the Atlantic about 500 miles southeast of St. John's, Newfoundland, a Wellfleet cliff was involved in the events of that memorable night. On that cliff stood a Marconi wireless telegraph station, built in 1902 and used to send the first transatlantic message from the United States to Europe in January 1903. On the evening of April 14, 1912 the Wellfleet station was busy relaying messages across the crisp, star-filled night air to the station at Cape Race on Newfoundland. These messages were mostly from family and friends of *Titanic*

Early twentieth century postcard depicting Wellfleet's Marconi wireless station, which received a distress call from the Titanic *in 1912. (J. Coogan collection)*

passengers, passed on from New York, as the mighty vessel approached North America on her well-publicized maiden voyage.

Also monitoring and perhaps preparing to pass on some of these messages from the Wellfleet station was radio operator Harold Cottam of the *Carpathia,* of the Cunard line. *Carpathia* was about 58 miles southeast and unaware of the disaster when Cottam sent the following message to the *Titanic* at 12:25 am: *"I say, old man, do you know there is a batch of messages coming through for you from MCC?"* The "MCC" refers to the Cape Cod station at Wellfleet ... Marconi Cape Cod.

The *Titanic's* senior radio operator, Jack Phillips, then sent back the following reply: *"Come at once. We have struck a berg. It's a CQD (Come Quick, Danger), old man. Position 41.46 N 50.14W."*

Cottam, in disbelief, and then perhaps considering that even an iceberg could not seriously damage such a large and mighty vessel, responded: *"Shall I tell my captain? Do you require assistance?"* Phillips' answer: *"Yes, come quick."* The messages from Cape Cod were soon forgotten.

A placard at the Marconi site mentions that MCC station did receive a distress call from *Titanic*. That message could have been received directly from *Titanic*, or else was passed on to the Cape Cod station from a ship at sea on that night - *Carpathia, Frankfort,* or *Mount Temple* – or perhaps even from Cape Race station. These messages would then have been forwarded on from Cape Cod to New York, thus informing the world of the drama unfolding in the middle of the Atlantic.

The Shipwreck that Became a Clubhouse

One of the more unusual wrecks occurring on Cape Cod involved three former schooners that were being towed as coal barges from Maine to Philadelphia during the spring of 1915. The ships were the *Tunnel Ridge*, the *Manheim*, and the *Coleraine*.

Apparently deciding not to avail himself of the newly opened Cape Cod Canal, the captain of the tugboat *Mars* set out from Bangor and took advantage of a following sea to make good time to the vicinity of Highland Light in Truro. But the weather went sour before he could get a good lineup on the beacon and, with light snow and fog falling, the tug was in danger of going into the breakers south of Head of the Meadow Beach in Truro.

Realizing that the three barges behind him were being pushed up on the beach by the wind and following sea, and they would drag his tug ashore with them, the tugboat captain cut the towline and powered offshore to safety. In saving his vessel, the captain seemed to have completely disregarded the fact that there were crewmen aboard each of the old schooners and his actions had abandoned them to their fate.

On the *Manheim*, Captain George Israel attempted to slow the barge's run into the breakers by dropping both anchors. The other two former sailing schooners, now with only bare masts, didn't attempt to slow their grounding and hit the beach and began to break apart. Only the rapid response by the lifesavers at Highland Station allowed the crews of these vessels to come ashore safely by breeches buoy. Eventually, the *Manheim* struck the bar and her crewmen were also taken off by the same method.

Spring tides on Cape Cod tend to be particularly high and all three barges ended well up on the beach. After an assessment, it was determined that only the *Manheim* had any chance of being re-floated. In order to get a line on her, the other two vessels had to be burned because they obstructed the seaward route of escape of the former schooner.

Before their destruction, local citizens were given the chance to salvage anything they could use from the two abandoned hulks. A group of Truro men led by E. Hayes Small removed the three deckhouses of the *Coleraine* and hauled them up the 100-foot cliffs near Highland Light. Reassembled, they became the clubhouse for the Highland Golf Club, certainly an unusual fate for a shipwreck.

Captain Israel and his crew spent the better part of a year living aboard the stranded *Manheim*. On April 4, 1916, the old schooner barge was re-floated and was once again hauling coal up the coast.

Henry Beston and the Montclair Wreck

During 1926 and 1927, naturalist writer Henry Beston spent a year alone at his small house on the dunes of Nauset, overlooking the majesty of the Atlantic Ocean, to observe and document the ebb and flow of life on the Great Beach. From those observations came the classic Cape Cod book, *The Outermost House,* published in 1928.

With the beginning section of his sixth chapter, Beston documents a terrible shipwreck that occurred just offshore from the Orleans Coast Guard Station on March 4, 1927, the three-masted schooner *Montclair.*

Departing from Halifax, Nova Scotia just four days earlier, the vessel's holds were full of laths - bundles of long pieces of wood. The vessel hit the shoals off Nauset in a storm and the waves broke her apart, spilling her cargo of wood into the turbulent seas. The seven crewmen remained clutching to the stern of the ship as the severed bow section was pushed toward shore. Large seas pounded the stern.

Soon, only two crewmen remained clinging to the stern as Coast Guardsmen from the Orleans station attempted to fire a rope over to the stricken vessel. One of the men slipped into the sea but was saved by the other crewman. Finally, with the rising tide and the relentless waves, the stern section was lifted free and cast toward shore close enough that lifesavers could reach the vessel with a line. The two men were then pulled to safety. According to Beston, one of the two men later died and *"the only survivor is going on with the sea ... He says it's all he knows."*

Chapter
7

Inventors, Opportunists & Entrepreneurs

The nineteenth and twentieth centuries saw ingenious Americans inventing new products designed to aid people in their day-to-day lives. Some of those inventors hailed from Cape Cod. In fact, Luther Childs Crowell from this peninsula is credited with 280 patents, placing him third behind only Eli Whitney and Thomas Edison on the invention "hit parade." One of his most popular inventions was a machine for manufacturing square bottom paper bags.

Dr. Samuel Pitcher of Hyannis developed the formula for an elixir, which he later sold for a sum of $10,000 to New York businessman Charles Fletcher in 1869. Fletcher renamed the elixir "Fletcher's Castoria" and made a fortune, for it became one of the best-selling homeopathic remedies of the nineteenth century.

Meanwhile, Edward Petow, also of Hyannis, perfected a method of applying a chemical, which was made from herring scales, to glass beads in order to produce artificial pearls. His Cape Cod

United Products Company was founded during the years of the First World War and enjoyed much success during the 1920s until the depression years of the 1930s put him out of business.

Other inventions by Cape Codders included improvements on machines used in the cranberry and fishing industries, advancement in sail technology and in steam engines, and even the creation of a state of the art commode!

Winter's Frigid Crop

Prior to the advent of electric refrigeration, our ancestors relied on caves and pits in the ground to keep food from spoiling. People in northern lands, where small ponds froze over during winter months, were more fortunate. They could remove ice from these ponds and store it away for warmer months. The ancient Greeks and Romans used snow and ice to cool their drinks. George Washington had a small icehouse at Mount Vernon. Thomas Jefferson had one at Monticello. Franklin D. Roosevelt even had one at his home in Hyde Park that was in use into the 1940s.

Ice harvesting in this country and on Cape Cod began in the seventeenth century. In those days, farmers would go out to a local pond and using pretty much nothing more than an axe would chip out enough ice for personal use. This evolved over time into community-wide efforts, and the arsenal of equipment evolved from an axe to over 60 tools specifically designed for various purposes.

People of the village would band together into a synchronized team to harvest a vast quantity of ice in a short amount of time, all to be stored in a nearby icehouse until warmer weather arrived. These houses were constructed of wood with both an outer and inner wall. The space between these two walls was about 12 inches thick, into which an insulation of salt hay was stuffed. With over 350 lakes and ponds across the Cape, icehouses dotted the landscape with most every village boasting one.

In Barnstable village, an icehouse rested on the shores of Coggins Pond, now called Hinckley's Pond. Another Barnstable icehouse was located on 10-acre Joshua's Pond in the village of Osterville where John Williams made deliveries. Four miles to the east, ice was also harvested from Simmons Pond in Hyannis. Yarmouth had a number of icehouses sprinkled across town, at James Pond, Dennis Pond, Sandy Pond, and two at Long Pond. A glance at the *1880 Atlas of Barnstable County* shows icehouses also located at Kelleys Pond in West Dennis, Schoolhouse Pond in Brewster, Smith Pond in West Brewster, Icehouse Pond in Orleans, and Jemima Pond in Eastham as well as at Pond Village in Truro.

Because Cape Cod's winters were rather mild, the ice harvesting season was very brief. Those in business considered themselves lucky if they had two cold winters in a row. In the early part of the twentieth century there were a series of harsh winters, yet a May 1902 article in *New England Magazine* entitled "Lakes of Cape Cod"

SANDY POND ICE CO.

This Ice is harvested on "Sandy Pond" a lake well-known on account of its pure spring water and is especially desirable for family use. Supplied regularly and promptly at wholesale and retail.

E. F. MAHER, Prop.

This advertisement appeared in the Barnstable Directory of 1895, published by J. H. Hogan Company, Quincy, Massachusetts. (William Brewster Nickerson Room Collection - Cape Cod Community College) stated that Cape lakes froze to no more than five or six inches in thickness. Yet, accounts of those who actually harvested ice on Cape Cod make mention of ice eight inches thick, with 12 inches achieved during extremely cold winters.

The harvest would begin sometime in January or February after a lengthy cold spell. Natural ice takes 10 to 14 days to freeze thoroughly. The thickness of the ice was determined using an instrument called a measuring iron. If thick enough to harvest, the ice surface was then prepared. First, any snow was removed using horse drawn scrapers and plows. Surprisingly, snow actually impedes ice production, serving as insulation against the winter chill.

Next, two lines at right angles, perpendicular to each other, were etched across the ice surface, and then scored to two or three inches deep with a horse-drawn marker. Accuracy was critical at this stage, for all the subsequent scorings would grow from these two lines.

The entire ice field was then marked off using a horse-drawn marker with two blades, one of which rested in the previous line cut into the ice thus producing parallel lines. This was repeated over and over until the field was marked in a checkerboard pattern of 22-inch blocks. These guide lines were then used to score the ice to a depth of two-thirds the ice thickness using plows pulled by horses.

A channel was cut from the icehouse out to the center of the pond. The first block of ice cut out of the channel would be sunk and pushed under the ice at the side of the channel in a procedure known as "sinking the header." Subsequent blocks from the channel were then moved toward the icehouse until a canal of open water stretched from the pick-up point at the shoreline to the middle of the ice field. Now the harvesting could begin.

Using five-foot long saws and instruments called breaking-off bars, the scored ice at the middle of the pond was separated from the field. A good worker could cut an inch of ice with each stroke of the saw. As the opening in the pond became larger, the ice was separated from the field in the form of large sheets containing perhaps 50 to 200 individual blocks. One man with a float hook could move these sheets, weighing upwards of 100 tons. Ice hooks and poles ranged from six to 20 feet long.

Men working on the moving ice sheet broke off blocks. These blocks were moved along toward the pick-up point where either a conveyer belt or a horse-pulled hoist transported them up and into the icehouse. Inside, workers positioned the blocks, leaving a couple of inches of space around each, and placing sawdust between each layer. The house would be filled to within a few feet of the peak, with salt hay placed atop for insulation.

Up north, where the winters were longer and colder, the harvest could take place over the course of a few weeks. On Cape, though, where weather was unpredictable and thaws more often, the harvest proceeded quickly toward completion and a full icehouse. Typically, this took two or three days of constant work, even continuing into the evening hours when there was a moon overhead.

Occasionally, a horse fell through the ice or a worker slipped near an opening and ended up in the frigid waters. Both horse and man would be removed from the water and treated to avoid hypothermia. When one considers the risks, the extreme cold, and the long hours of laborious work, the 50 cents per hour earned during the early years of the twentieth century didn't seem like a lot. But work was scarce on Cape Cod in the winter and workers felt fortunate to have a paying job.

Mechanization arrived on the icy ponds just after the turn of the century with gasoline-powered saws capable of doing the work of four or five horses. The power saw could cut 12 inches into the ice, saving time and energy. The machines were expensive, though, and some small operators continued to use the horse-drawn methods well into the twentieth century.

Icehouses were typically built out in the open, away from tree cover. This was done to keep the house dry, as dampness is the worst condition in which to attempt to store ice. In the mid-nineteenth century, a 10-foot x 10-foot house provided adequate ice storage space for an average Cape Cod family. A ton of ice took up just less than 50 square feet.

Ten inches of sand formed the floor of the icehouse, providing drainage for the melting ice. Some icehouses, or at least the roofs, were painted white to reflect the sun's rays. Besides sawdust and salt hay, seaweed and pine needles were also used as insulation.

Even the most efficient houses saw a 10 to 30 percent ice shrinkage rate.

Beginning in May the iceman made his daily rounds, making deliveries around the village in his wagon. His day started early, before sunrise, as he hitched up his horse and stocked his wagon full of ice. In 1900, the delivery of 100 pounds of ice per week cost about two dollars. Customers placed an "ice card" in their window indicating to the driver how much ice was needed that day - usually in increments of 25, 50, 75, and 100 pounds. The mid-Cape had a number of ice deliverymen. E.F. Maher ran his Sandy Pond Ice Company, which advertised ice "harvested on Sandy Pond, a lake well-known on account of its pure spring water and is especially desirable for family use." The *1890 Yarmouth Directory* displays an advertisement for John Usher, Jr. of Wharf Lane in Yarmouthport who delivered his "Pure Pond Ice" around the village. The *1890 Bourne Directory* lists four ice dealers, including H.T. Handy & Son on Centre Street in Cataumet. Eight ice dealers are listed in the *Falmouth Directory* while Marshall L. Adams on Commercial Street in Provincetown appears in both the *1880 Atlas of Barnstable County* and the *1890 Barnstable County Directory*.

Around 1913, the first electric refrigerators appeared. In the 1920s natural ice production began to wane and by the late-1930s the harvesting of ice on Cape Cod ponds and on ponds and lakes around the country had pretty much ended. Some Cape Codders did continue to harvest pond ice into the 1940s, including Anson Howes at Scargo Lake in Dennis.

Today, ponds and lakes across Cape Cod in winter offer a pretty view and a spot for ice-skating. The labors of past generations are now largely forgotten. No longer do men saw ice and stock houses with winter's frigid crop ... with thoughts of how nice a cold glass of lemonade will taste come July and August.

Not Just Another Smith

The Smith name is a pretty common one just about anywhere. But Stephen Smith of Barnstable was no ordinary Smith!

Born in Barnstable near Coggins Pond (now Hinckley's Pond) in

August of 1805, Smith apprenticed himself as a teenager to a Sandwich master wood craftsman known as "Cabinetmaker Swift." The young boy showed an excellent aptitude for woodworking and by the age of 21 he was skilled enough to go off on his own. He made his way to Boston where he took employment with Solomon Lord, a well-known city cabinetmaker. Within two years he left this enterprise and went into partnership with a Hilliard Smith as a clockmaker. Eventually he bought out his partner and opened his own business specializing in all manner of fine cabinetry.

Even with increasing success in Boston, Stephen Smith did not forget his Barnstable roots. He visited with his Cape Cod family often and in 1830 he married a local girl named Liza D. Lothrop. It was shortly after his marriage that Smith's most revolutionary idea came to fruition.

The decade of the 1830s was a time of expanding commercial activity in America and there was a growth in counting houses and merchant offices. In every office was a standard flat-topped desk. Mountains of invoices, ledgers, and account books cluttered these desks without any sense of organization. Smith seized on the idea of creating a desk with cubbyholes that could be used for organizing paperwork. He built up the backside of the desk so that there was a sort of walled organizer beyond the working surface. The final innovation was a sliding lid that could be pulled down over the whole space and locked. This was the first rolltop desk.

He patented his idea and began production of the new product in his shop at 44 Cornhill Street in Boston. In part due to the business panic of 1837 his invention was slow to take off, but by the early 1840s Smith's rolltop desks began to sell so well that he became a very wealthy man. He purchased large amounts of property in his native Barnstable and expanded his Boston shop to meet the demand for his desks. Within a decade his rolltop desks could be found all over the United States and had been exported to many countries around the world.

He spent summers at his Barnstable home where he had extensive gardens. Smith also involved himself in the improvement of his adopted home of Boston, building Minot Hall and Concord Hall, and serving on several city committees for development of the South End. He made his residence in Newton when he was not in Barnstable.

Stephen Smith died of a stroke in April of 1875. His death notice in the *Barnstable Patriot* noted that he was a benefactor to his native town and "he had many warm friends who esteemed him for his genial disposition, generous heart and kindly nature." Had he lived only a year longer Smith would have seen his rolltop desk take a bronze medal for excellence in office furniture design and a $1,000 prize at the 1876 Philadelphia Exhibition.

The Man Who Challenged Cunard

Edward Knight Collins was born in Truro in 1802. During a brilliant career in the transatlantic shipping business he saw his fortunes soar to the point that he presented a serious challenge to Britain's famous ship owner, Samuel Cunard.

At one time in the mid-nineteenth century his Collins Line ran some of the most modern steamships of the era and his enterprise set new standards for comfort, speed, and efficiency. And yet his meteoric rise turned into ashes following a series of ship disasters leaving him to die a forgotten man in 1878.

Collins began his career at sea as a typical New England coasting skipper. Eventually, he gravitated to New York City where he joined a partnership with his father Israel G. Collins. In 1835, the young entrepreneur made his first move to buy out the partnership of rival shippers Foster and Hutton. He established his own New York to New Orleans "Dramatic Line" and soon dominated the cotton trade between these two ports with five good-sized vessels. By 1837, Collins entered the New York to Liverpool trade with three new and fast sailing ships skippered by respected Cape Cod shipmasters. A year later he launched the clipper *Roscius*, at the time the largest American merchant ship afloat. The ship was commanded by his uncle, Captain John Collins, and it became the flagship of the fleet.

The success of the business through the 1840s was capped when Collins was given a contract from the U.S. government to carry the mail across the Atlantic for $385,000 a year. With this guaranteed subsidy, Collins secured financing to build a fleet of four steamships that would be the best in the trade. As if he anticipated controlling the trade routes of the entire world, he named the vessels after four major world sea regions - *Arctic, Atlantic, Baltic,* and *Pacific.* Unlike the dependable but stodgy Cunard vessels, the Collins line steamers featured well-appointed dining rooms, carpeted staterooms, and even French cuisine. These speedy vessels were virtual "floating palaces" and boasted steam heat and indoor plumbing. The dining salon of the steamer *Atlantic,* for example, measured 60 feet by 12 feet and the lounge was even larger.

While these were heady days for the Collins Line, there were elements of concern. Competition was fierce for freight and passengers in the transatlantic trade. The British and French carved out major sectors of the market and had larger subsidies from their governments. Success in the trade was built on optimistic views of continuous expansion and the availability of hefty bank financing. The financial picture was precarious as the 1850s began. Collins was operating on a razor thin margin that gave little room for the unexpected. He felt he was in the clear when the government increased his mail subsidy to $850,000 and he pumped the additional money into the planning of his super ship, the 4,000-ton steamer *Adriatic.*

In September of 1854, the *Arctic* ran into the French steamer *Vesta* off Newfoundland and was lost with 300 to 400 passengers. Among those who went down with the ship were Collins' wife and two of his four children. Compounding what was certainly a terrible personal blow, there were stories of abandonment of survivors by the *Arctic's* crew. The reputation of the Collins Line came under attack. Two years later, the *Pacific,* commanded by Yarmouth's Asa Eldridge, was lost without a trace in the ice floes of the North Atlantic. This happened while Collins was engaged in building the *Adriatic.*

With half his fleet at the bottom of the sea and overextended in his construction financing, Collins woke up one morning to learn that Congress had withdrawn the mail contract that kept the company afloat. New York rival Cornelius Vanderbilt used his considerable political influence and the misfortunes of the Collins Line to get the government grant for himself. With his cash flow suddenly cut off, Collins was forced to sell the completed *Adriatic* to British interests and he declared bankruptcy. The two remaining Collins steamers were sold at sheriff's auction, bringing but a fraction of what was needed to pay off his debts. He lost his 300-acre New York estate, Larchmont Manor, and retreated to his small Ohio farm with his dreams, if not his fortune, intact.

For some years after the fortunes of maritime commerce turned against him, Edward Knight Collins attempted to re-enter the shipping business. He also tried coal and iron mining without success. Always dogged by the mid-century collapse of his shipping enterprise, Collins was unable to secure the necessary credit to start over. The man who once challenged Samuel Cunard and who had been an international celebrity, died in obscurity on January 22, 1878.

Caleb Chase - Cape Cod's "Coffee Baron"

Born the youngest of 17 children in 1831, Caleb Chase of Harwich chose not to follow his brothers into the seafaring trades.

Instead, he joined a Boston dry-goods wholesale firm of Anderson, Sargent & Co. During the Civil War he became a partner in his own company, Carr, Chase, and Raymond. In 1878, the firm became Chase and Sanborn, the largest coffee import firm in America at the time. The company was the first to pack coffee in sealed cans and had branches in Montreal and Chicago. Chase's partner in the venture was Charles Sanborn, a Maine man with family connections to Cape Cod. The two men became wealthy and Mr. Chase, now known as "Colonel Chase," established his summer home "Good Cheer" on the Herring River in West Harwich.

Despite his wealth, Caleb Chase considered himself to be a common man in his native Harwich, spending every summer there. He became a great benefactor to the town and was known as a man who would pay off the mortgages of widows of men lost at sea. In 1903, he presented the Harwich Exchange Building as a gift to the town after retiring its $40,000 mortgage. At his death in December of 1908, his estate was valued in excess of two million dollars! A number of scholarships and trust funds were established in his name that still provide help to people in the mid-Cape area.

The story of Caleb Chase would not be complete without the strange circumstance that brought his name back to prominence in the 1990s. After many years of dormancy, the old Chase and Sanborn coffee logo was reintroduced by the Nestle Company in a move to evoke some nostalgia for its coffee line. The graphics experts, however, mistakenly switched the identities of Mr. Chase and Mr. Sanborn on the new label. In November of 1992, Harwich Historical Society member Patricia Buck had the keen eye to notice the error and she alerted Brooks Academy Museum Director Beverly Thacher. Mrs. Thacher wrote to the company and the mistake was eventually corrected. In gratitude, the embarrassed Nestle Company sent dozens of cases of coffee with the proper labels to the Historical Society. As for the incorrect labels, they have become collectors' items - almost like misprinted stamps. But at least the new "old" labels now have Caleb Chase once again in his rightful place.

The South Yarmouth Wire Factory

Hard by the western shore of Bass River off Kelley Street is the site of the old South Yarmouth Wire Factory. More formally known as the American Metallic Fabric Company, the business was started in 1885 by Samuel D. Kelley to produce woven brass, and later bronze and stainless steel cloth. For almost a century it was a mainstay of the local industry of South Yarmouth.

Sam Kelley was a local Yarmouth boy who had gone to Boston to make his fortune. He was a successful architect in the city and designed a number of buildings that still are part of the Hub skyline. Feeling that he wanted to return to his roots, he decided to bring a steam-powered industry to his hometown. With $25,000 in stock, Kelley built a factory that occupied about 4,000 square feet of space with a number of steam-powered weaving looms.

In the beginning, the wire mesh was used to screen pulp fiber that went into the paper making process. As the business grew, it supplied paper mill wire cloth to mills from Maine to Florida. A large dock was built on Bass River so coal schooners could supply the factory's steam power plant. The steady thump of the looms and the punctual noon whistle became part of the life of the small village.

Kelley and his brother Seth remained in control of the business until the first decade of the twentieth century, after which it was sold to a wire company in Springfield. The plant continued operations into the early 1930s when production was suspended temporarily during the Depression years. In 1940, Roger Edwards purchased the factory and modernized it. With his son Robert as vice president, and later under the direction of his grandson, Roger, the company was successful through much of the 1950s and 1960s.

But as with many small businesses occupying specific niche markets, the company lost market share and was forced to close in the 1970s. The once flourishing plant lay vacant for almost 20 years when it was finally torn down in the late 1990s.

The Captain and the Baby Carriage

There are tales of sea captains who become expert scrimshanders, producing beautiful scrimshaw works on the teeth and bones of whales. Other captains passed the time at sea doing needlework and even crochet. But it is believed that only one sea captain worked on designs for a newfangled baby carriage.

Henry Kittredge, in writing his book, *Shipmasters of Cape Cod*, made some notes indicating that Captain Valentine Doane of Harwich (1804-1896) had invented a new type of baby carriage. Actually, rather than the father, it was the son, Valentine Doane, Jr. (1833-1911) who was the inventor of this new baby carriage.

Young Mr. Doane did not follow in the footsteps of his seagoing father. After a few years at sea, he became a fish dealer with his father at the Marsh Bank wharf in Harwichport, and later in Portsmouth, New Hampshire. He was also involved in several manufacturing ventures. In later life he returned to the family homestead in West Harwich where he became a respected citizen.

In 1888, he applied for a patent for an improved version of a baby carriage. As the line drawing would indicate, it was a complex piece of machinery and the patent application was four pages in length in describing its operation. Doane was issued patent #393,298 on

November 20, 1888. Nothing seemed to have come of the new style baby carriage and the invention rated only a brief mention in the *Harwich Independent* newspaper. But as it has been said that necessity is often the mother of invention, so it appears to have been the case with Valentine Doane, Jr. – he was the father of 10 children!

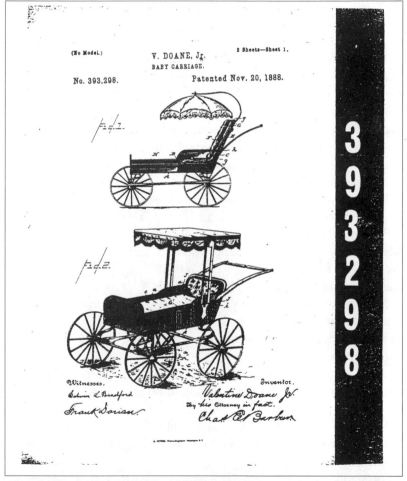

Plans for Captain Valentine Doane, Jr.'s baby carriage, patent number 393,298. (Boston Public Library – public records/U.S. patents section)

Banana Bonanza

The nation island of Jamaica, with a quarter of its labor force working in the field of agriculture, lists bananas as one of its chief crops and major exports. That industry and its century-long banana trade can be traced to the efforts of a Cape Cod man who saw an opportunity within those slippery yellow peels.

Arriving at Jamaica in 1870 on board the schooner *Telegraph* to pick up a cargo of bamboo was Captain Lorenzo Dow Baker of Wellfleet. As he was making his pickup he had his men take on a supply of bananas. His plan was to transport them north to Boston to see if there was any interest in the fruit. Yet, by the time the *Telegraph* had arrived only as far north as the Carolinas the fruit spoiled and was cast overboard.

The very next year Baker was in Jamaica again. This time he took a supply of green bananas and was successful in delivering them to Boston before they had a chance to spoil. The fruit was well received and he knew he was on to something good. The wheels began to turn in his head. He established the L. D. Baker Company to move cargoes of fruit from tropical places to American ports. That company became the Boston Fruit Company, and later, United Fruit Company.

For a number of years Baker split his time between his Cape Cod home in Wellfleet and his adopted second home on Jamaica. In Wellfleet he built the Chequesset Inn in 1885, a grand hotel that was situated out over the waters at Wellfleet Harbor. Meanwhile, in Jamaica he dabbled in ways of promoting the island and its exports to off-island interests, bringing economic prosperity both as a tourist destination and a grower of exotic fruits and useable natural resources.

Jamaica never forgot the man who helped to improve their economy. In 1905, a ceremony was held on the island where the 65-year old Baker was presented with a silver service as a token of thanks for his efforts. It was stated at the ceremony that he did more for the island in 30 years "than the British Empire in three hundred years."

Lorenzo Dow Baker *slipped* the tethers of earth for the heavenly sphere in 1908.

Skunks!

Cape Codders are an enterprising lot. For over three centuries, residents of the Cape have figured out a way to wrest a living from an often difficult and unforgiving environment. Schemes have ranged from the very practical to the bizarre. But of all of the ways of making money on Cape Cod, perhaps the most unusual was the commercial exploitation of the lowly skunk.

At the turn of the twentieth century the Provincetown Skunk Works was started. Animals were raised for their fur as well as for their meat. Pelts brought as much as five dollars each. Around the same period a skunk farm was developed in South Yarmouth. Local residents were encouraged to trap the odorous creatures and bring them to the farm where they were purchased and later sold for their fur.

Don Sparrow, in his book *Growing Up on Cape Cod*, tells of trapping skunks in Eastham during the Depression years using a good "skunking dog" and the benefit of a full moon to catch the nocturnal animals. Prices for "quarter stripers," mostly all black fur pelts, could command as much as $2.50 in the Boston market, not bad in a time when a dollar went a very long way. Sparrow gives credit to his neighbor Charlie Escobar as being the "King of the Skunkers." Escobar was skilled enough to be able to sneak up and grab the tail of a skunk, quickly lifting the creature off the ground before it could spray him – at least most of the time anyway. Sparrow admits that the "Skunker King" had a very strong aroma that stayed with the intrepid hunter for most of the season.

On the north side of Yarmouth, at around the same time, John Silver sold skunk oil that he claimed cured everything from a baby's cough to rheumatism. He once claimed that his product was applied to the crippled hands of an old woman who suffered from arthritis and within a week she was threading needles! Reportedly, his enterprise was located off Willow Street not far from the train station. It would be assumed that he had few close neighbors. Asked if he ever got "skunked" while trapping the animals, Silver admitted that indeed he had.

"Yes Sir," he said. "I got it right in the eyes. But, mind you, after that happened my sight was immediately improved. Never saw better in my life than I did that night."

That his business was no mere whimsy can be seen in the fact that Silver continued to sell his product for almost 40 years and, while he never got rich, his oil was sought after by people from one end of the Cape to the other.

The Ambergris King

One of the curious by-products of the whaling industry is the substance called ambergris. For many years it became an important article of commerce, particularly in the production of perfume where it acted as a fixing agent for the perfume scent. Because of its short supply and its value in the perfume industry, ambergris was one of the highest priced products of the sea, selling for as much as five hundred dollars a pound. In terms of return per pound value, ambergris was actually more valuable than gold.

Of all the people who ever traded in this substance, there was only one individual who ever claimed to be the "Ambergris King of America." That person was a Provincetown man named David Conwell Stull. When he died in February of 1926 at the age of 81, Stull was the acknowledged ambergris expert in the United States.

In the declining years of American whaling, between 1895 and 1925, Mr. Stull was a familiar sight along the wharves of New Bedford and Boston whenever a whaling ship would arrive and report a supply of ambergris aboard. Stull would grade the substance for its purity by comparing it to a small supply that he kept in the setting of a ring that he wore on his left hand. Once the appraisal of quality was made, Stull would bid on the ambergris and eventually transfer it at a handsome profit to his overseas contacts in the perfume business.

It is said that in the history of the ambergris trade only about a ton and a half of the substance ever came to the market and David Stull was the purchaser of about half of that amount. Sometimes potential customers came to his shop on Commercial Street with materials that they believed to be ambergris.

"Yes, all kinds of common and uncommon things are sent by mail, or persons bring them into my shop at Provincetown, feeling sure they are ambergris," Stull noted in one account. "Here are some of the articles: wood pulp, fungus that grows in sea water, paraffin, sealing wax, soap, slush, or soap grease; lost or thrown overboard from some ship, and many other objects that are not ambergris."

Mr. Stull was also interested in the oil found in the heads of Blackfish, which he refined into high quality lubricating oil for delicate machinery. Many of the lighthouses on the East Coast used his oil products to ensure the smooth operation of the machinery. The oil was particularly prized because it would not freeze in cold weather. In his advertisements for his watch and clock establishment he claimed to have "the finest oil on earth."

Falmouth - America's Mushroom Capital

In 1911, the enterprise known as Falmouth Mushroom Cellars, Inc. began doing business near the corner of Gifford Street and Morse Road. The 18-acre complex featured its own electric generating plant that allowed the growing rooms to maintain a steady year round temperature of 58 degrees. The main building was, for some strange reason, designed in the style of a Spanish mission and even featured a bell tower that served as a water tower. Several outbuildings and greenhouses were constructed with plans for more as the business grew.

The company quickly prospered and by 1914 it was not only producing a large number of high quality fresh mushrooms for the Boston market, but boasted that it was the largest commercial mushroom industry in the world. It claimed that its mushrooms were as large as five inches across! But just as quickly as its success had come, so came the company's rapid demise. In the fall of 1916, the mushroom end of the business succumbed to an uncontrollable blight. With the United States poised to enter World War I, the company shifted emphasis to the canning side of the business. Tomatoes, beets, and beans were preserved and shipped from the plant. Canning kept over 100 workers busy during the war years and provided a good market for the fruits and vegetables of upper Cape farmers.

After the war, however, fresh produce replaced the canned vegetable market and the company closed for good in 1922. The property was purchased by John Davis of Falmouth Heights who used the large cement buildings for a piggery. Today, as well-heeled diners enjoy the ambiance of the nearby Coonamessett Inn, there is nothing to mark what was once the largest commercial mushroom business in the entire world.

Hyannis' House of Wax

A thriving Cape Cod business that is still around today had its humble beginnings in the kitchen of a Hyannis woman.

Mabel Baker began creating hand-dipped candles around 1908 as a hobby, giving them to family members and friends as birthday and Christmas presents. The gifts were well received and the local popularity of the candles grew. Seizing on this popularity, her husband, Walter, soon carried them at his Hyannis department store. Sales of the candles were strong enough for Walter and Mabel to hire a crew to pick the bayberries necessary to create the wax.

Eventually, Walter sold his store in order to dedicate one hundred percent of his time and effort toward candle production. In 1921, they built a factory in Hyannis and by 1925 sales had reached one million candles annually. To keep up with demand, the Bakers employed over 40 workers to produce the candles using both hand-dipping methods and molds. They also hired over 20 salesmen to sell the candles across New England. Production increased from a few thousand to 10,000 per day, decades later jumping to over 100,000 per day with the development of automated methods.

The company produced a wide assortment of candles and also produced what they referred to as "character candles" depicting characters from American history. Candles have been shipped all over the globe, and today the company remains one of the largest producers of candles in the world. Nowadays, Colonial Candle of Cape Cod can still be found at the site of the original factory, and is a necessary stop for any Hyannis tourists looking to bring home an aromatic reminder of their Cape Cod visit.

Chapter
8

Revolt & Rebellion

Despite geographic isolation, Cape Codders did not escape the challenges that faced the colonies and the nation in the eighteenth and nineteenth centuries. As the larger questions of American independence, and later slavery and secession, were being debated, residents of Barnstable County took their own stands.

In meetinghouses and taverns, these issues sparked lively debate and occasionally even physical confrontation. Local patriots like James Otis, Jr. and Nathaniel Freeman not only brought ideas of change into Cape forums, but they also became important leaders in the growing movement for separation from Great Britain. Certainly, Cape Cod was no backwater when it came to making an impact on the Revolutionary War. With British warships patrolling the waters around the Cape, residents experienced firsthand the serious consequences of the struggle for liberty and freedom. By war's end, Cape Cod was economically devastated, but triumphant – and free.

During the middle of the nineteenth century, the growing abolition movement had, as it had done to the rest of the country, polarized much of Cape Cod. While there were some strong anti-slavery advocates on the Cape, including a few who openly moved to assist escaped slaves in their flight to freedom, just as many other local residents saw the issue as unworthy of support and feelings ran high on both sides. But when rebel gunners fired on Fort Sumter in 1861 there was almost a unanimous show of support for the Union cause. Hundreds of Cape men volunteered for service in the Federal Army and Navy and many lost their lives in the struggle. By 1865, when the Civil War ended, Cape Cod was confidently entering the industrial age.

A "No" Vote on Independency!

In the decisive days before the adoption of the Declaration of Independence, a number of Cape Cod towns held town meetings to discuss the adoption or rejection of the document.

The town of Harwich held its meeting on June 17, 1776 and voted that its representatives to the General Court should support independence. Wellfleet endorsed the document the same week. Despite its exposed position on the outer Cape, Truro voted independence on June 18, 1776. Two days later in Yarmouth, the citizens voted unanimously "that the inhabitants of the town of Yarmouth do declare a state of independence of the King of Great Britain, agreeably to a late resolve of the General Court, if in case the wisdom of Congress should see proper to do it."

In Barnstable, however, there was considerable support for the position of the Crown. As the shire town and the birthplace of the patriot James Otis, Jr., one would think that the Cape's largest and most influential town would have been a leader in the adoption of the Declaration of Independence. Indeed, the 1774 march to Barnstable of the "Body of the People," a group of patriots who strongly objected to the King's tampering with the jury system, indicated that there was a substantial group of citizens who took issue with England's colonial rule.

But some wealthy and influential Tories, led by Edward Bacon, so intimidated the voters at the June 25 meeting that a large number refused even to vote on the question of supporting the declaration. The "rump" remainder tallied 30 citizens in favor of independence and 35 against it. Independence was defeated. Barnstable was only the second town in all of New England, the other being Ridgefield, Connecticut, that failed to produce a positive vote for independence.

The next day, a vigorous protest letter was sent to Boston, signed by 23 citizens of Barnstable who demanded another vote and who pledged their support for independence. They wrote "to let posterity know that there were a few in this town who dared stand forth in favor of an injured and oppressed country . . . and it is a matter of great grief to us that the Cause of Liberty is treated with such indignity by some of the inhabitants of the town of Barnstable." The after-the-fact letter mattered little to the General Court who stripped Barnstable of its representation in that legislative body until the war was almost over.

Perhaps what is even more curious is that despite the discontent that followed the vote against the Declaration of Independence, Edward Bacon, the chief Loyalist opponent of the document, was re-elected to the General Court as Barnstable's representative. He was denied a seat by the General Court in 1778 and yet he was re-elected again in 1780 and finally, despite his unfailing Tory sentiments, he was allowed to take his seat in the legislature. The voters of Barnstable apparently saw no inconsistency in continuing to support and elect a representative during the war that actively opposed the break with England.

The "Crocker Quarrel"

During the period leading up to the Declaration of Independence from Great Britain, the village of Barnstable was a village in conflict. Positions on the matter of independence were split down the middle with Whigs tending their fields and digging their shellfish side by side with Tories. It is understandable that these Whigs and Tories of the same village did not share the same opinions of the day's events, but there is evidence to suggest that even the Whigs in Barnstable did not see eye-to-eye with one another either.

Barnstable at that time was a caldron of conflicting thought. The 1774 march against the courthouse seemed to suggest that the cause for independence was firmly rooted in the shire town, yet as presented in the section above that was not the case when the issue was put to a vote.

Events taking place just one month before the vote seem to shed some light on just how divided even the Whigs themselves were at that time. In fact, the account of historian Amos Otis, who wrote *Genealogical Notes of Barnstable Families*, indicates that there were four divisions in the Cape town – passionate Whigs, moderate Whigs, passionate Tories, and moderate Tories. No matter which camp you were in, you had enemies in the other three.

Town records for May 1776 reference an address to be made by Colonel James Otis, the father of the Patriot. Apparently the esteemed Colonel was invited to speak before the assembly, but it was voted that they would not hear an apology on the "Crocker Quarrel," nor on the "Abigail Freeman affair." The apologies refer to two events that had recently taken place on the streets of the village.

The Crocker Tavern of Barnstable, scene of the 1776 "Crocker Quarrel." (J. Sheedy photo)

The "Quarrel" in question occurred during a training exercise as Colonel Joseph Otis, brother of the Patriot, and Colonel Nathaniel Freeman ran the men through some drills. The soldiers snubbed their commanding officers by refusing to follow their orders. Otis, an ardent Whig, immediately blamed the Crocker boys for the insubordinate action, barking at moderate Whig Captain Sam Crocker, "The Crockers are at the bottom of this!" After a further exchange of words Otis swung his cane at Crocker and all hell broke loose.

Meanwhile, Colonel Freeman took on Cornelius Crocker, who owned the nearby Crocker Tavern. The argument between the two men went from the street and into the tavern, where an old-fashioned sword fight took place. Apparently Crocker was struck a number of times until his brother Elijah arrived with rifle in hand. Fortunately, the fight was broken up before anyone was killed.

At about the same time as the Crocker Quarrel another event took place in the village – the tarring and feathering of the widow Abigail Freeman. Described in Donald Trayser's *Barnstable: Three Centuries of a Cape Cod Town* as "an outspoken shrewish Tory," the widow Nabby, as she was called, was taken from her bed in the middle of the night and hauled out into the street. Her fierce Tory stance had angered many of the village's Whigs and made her a target for their aggression. In what was to become the only recorded case in Barnstable, and probably on all of Cape Cod, the old woman was tarred and feathered and then carried around the streets on a rail. It was certainly a low point in Barnstable's struggle for independence, to perform such deeds against an old woman.

Tempers cooled over the months that followed, although the occasional toppling of a Liberty Pole reminded residents that differing views prevailed in the Yankee village of Barnstable.

Cape Cod's Biggest Revolutionary Prize

Cape Cod can point to a proud history of fighting for the cause of revolution against the Crown. Toward that end, this peninsula produced an unlikely cast of heroes who risked all for a fragile ideal called independence.

In fact, the Cape's involvement in the struggle for independence from Great Britain began years before the Declaration of Independence was written and a decade before British soldiers fired on an angry crowd at what became the Boston Massacre. For instance, at Boston's Old State House, in February 1761, West Barnstable native James Otis, Jr., delivered an impassioned speech against the British Writs of Assistance. Among those who heard the speech was young Boston lawyer John Adams who would later write: "Mr. Otis' oration breathed into this nation the breath of life ... then and there was the first scene of the first act of the opposition to the arbitrary claims of Great Britain ... American independence was then and there born."

Otis' younger sister, Mercy Otis Warren, was also a champion for the Patriots' cause. A friend of many important political figures of the day, including John Adams, his wife Abigail, and John Hancock, Mercy penned political satire that lampooned the British establishment. Her plays and poems, many of which were published in the Patriot newspapers of the day, provided revolutionary propaganda to fan the flames her brother had earlier lit.

Yet, Cape Cod's involvement in the war would come closer to home. In fact, in 1778 it would come to the shoals off Truro, marking the first victory by Cape rebels against the Crown. The victory would amount to the Cape's biggest prize of the war, though the local militia would receive a great deal of assistance by way of Mother Nature's fury.

On November 2, 1778, the 64-gun British warship *HMS Somerset*, a participant in the Battle of Bunker Hill three years earlier, was having difficulty navigating the treacherous bars and shoals off Truro's east shore. Using Provincetown Harbor as its base of operation, *Somerset* was harassing the Cape towns for months, her crew stealing provisions and otherwise making life miserable for those living along the coastline. But the mighty ship, carrying several hundred of King George's finest soldiers, was no match for the foul New England weather, nor the lurking sand bars that threatened to snatch unsuspecting mariners who wandered too close to Cape Cod's outer shore. Eventually,

Statue of Patriot Mercy Otis Warren outside the county courthouse in Barnstable village. (A. Sheedy photo)

Somerset hit bottom and wrecked near the site of the future
Highland Light, her hull hopelessly hung up on the sands and
her bulk pounded by rough surf.

It is believed that perhaps as many as 200 men were drowned.
The number of survivors according to accounts of the day
amounted to anywhere from 300 to nearly 500 men. Their commander, a Captain Ourry (also spelled Orrey or Aurey), surrendered to Truro selectman Isaiah Atkins. The British prisoners were
then made the responsibility of Captain Enoch Hallett of
Yarmouth. Over the days and weeks that followed, the captured
soldiers were marched by Captain Hallett, using the services of
various Cape militias, from Truro to Boston where they were later
exchanged for American prisoners of war.

As for the wreck of the *HMS Somerset*, she was picked over by
locals until most of her treasures were confiscated. By the time the
General Court decided what to do with the wreck and her contents
there was nothing left. Her hull was burned down to the waterline
and the rest of her became sanded in, her remains buried in the
Cape's shipwreck graveyard. Over the course of centuries her ribs
were exhumed on the beach from time to time by the tides. And a
number of homes on Cape Cod today boast a piece of wood from
this eighteenth century British warship that once lobbed cannonballs during the Battle of Bunker Hill.

Enoch Crosby - Revolutionary Spy

He was a Patriot and a behind the scenes contributor to the
winning of American independence. His exploits became the
inspiration for one of the great nineteenth century American
adventure novels. He is also virtually unknown in the Cape Cod
town of his birth.

Enoch Crosby is perhaps the most obscure of the many Revolutionary War personalities who came from Cape Cod. He was born
in Harwich on Christmas day in 1749 to Thomas and Elizabeth
Crosby. Some references give his birth as January 4, 1750, which
might be due to the adoption of the modern calendar. Regardless
of his actual birth date, Crosby was a valuable and unsung spy for

the American cause.

Not much is known about Crosby's short stay in Harwich. One reference has the family moving to Carmel, New York around the time of his third birthday. He left that home by age 16 and was apprenticed as a shoemaker. At around age 21 he migrated to Danbury, Connecticut. By the outset of the Revolution he set out on foot to enlist in the American Army. To keep himself in food and shelter, he stopped in towns along the way to repair the shoes of local people. As he worked, he listened to the conversations of British sympathizers and picked up useful information and passed it on to the American side. Patriot officials convinced him that he could be of more value to the cause of independence if he continued to use his profession as a convenient means to spy on Loyalists throughout New York and New England.

With the perfect disguise of an itinerant journeyman shoemaker, Crosby traveled frequently between Connecticut, New York, Massachusetts, and even as far as Vermont. Many Loyalists were identified, particularly in the so-called "neutral ground" of Westchester County, New York, and their plans compromised by his observations. Eventually, Tory suspicions about Crosby's real intentions made his mission too dangerous and brought his career as a spy to a close. Still wanting to make a contribution, Crosby enlisted in the American Army and served until the war's end.

There is a record of an Enoch Crosby publishing intentions to marry a Bethia Rogers of Orleans in October of 1800, but it is not clear that this is the same man or if he had returned temporarily to Harwich during that time. It appears unlikely that he maintained his Cape Cod connection. He was content to settle on a farm that he shared with his brother near Carmel, New York. There he lived until his death in June of 1835.

James Fenimore Cooper heard about Enoch Crosby's wartime intelligence work and used the story line in one of his best-selling novels, *The Spy*, which was written in 1821. Crosby's character took the form of itinerant peddler Harvey Birch. Like his fictional counterpart, Crosby had been occasionally stigmatized during the war years by his seemingly close association with British sympathizers and despite his army service he faced occasional criticism as an alleged one-time foe of liberty.

In 1827, Crosby was in New York City and was invited to view a play based on *The Spy*. When the audience was made aware that he was there, they gave him a standing ovation. It was only at this time that Crosby's quiet contributions to the cause of American independence were publicly recognized.

Yet, that recognition has never reached the place of his birth. There is no monument in Harwich that mentions Enoch Crosby and few are aware of his connection to the town.

Cape's Last Revolutionary War Veteran

In 1856, Cape Cod lost its last link to the Revolutionary War when Isaac Snow of Orleans died at the age of 97.

Enlisting at the age of 17, Snow joined up with General Washington's Army in Boston in the spring of 1776. He was very eager to fight for his country, spending the early part of his enlistment building a crude fortress at Dorchester Heights under the command of Captain Solomon Higgins of Eastham. The British attacked the Heights with cannon fire, but without success. In fact, Snow and others retrieved the cannonballs fired to use later against the British.

Snow witnessed the British evacuation of Boston that he had helped bring about with his efforts at Dorchester Heights. After his three-month enlistment he went home to Orleans, but soon reenlisted and headed back to Boston. After a time, he joined the crew of the vessel *Defense* and headed out to sea. Though a good many of the crew suffered from smallpox, *Defense* engaged a British ship and was victorious, carrying its prize back to Boston. Later, while again at sea, he was captured by the British and put upon a prison ship. After a time he escaped, walking by foot through Portugal, Spain, and finally into France where he joined a French fleet bound for America.

In 1780, he served on the *Resolution*, a 10-gun brig. Again the British captured him, this time sending him to Old Mill Prison in Plymouth, England where he remained for nearly two years before a prisoner exchange set him free. With the war's conclusion, Snow returned to Orleans to become a cobbler and a miller. In 1797, when the town broke away from Eastham and was incorporated, he was a strong supporter of the French name "Orleans," perhaps due to his strong dislike of the English and as a token of thanks to the French who sided with the Americans during the war and had delivered him safely home after his first incarceration.

Snow was still young enough to pitch in during the next war with Britain, helping to train the local militia during the War of 1812. He finally retired and lived off his war pension for the remaining years of his life, dying as the Cape's last Revolutionary War veteran.

The Ransom of the Saltworks

During the War of 1812, British warships controlled the waters around Cape Cod. In addition to the regular job of commerce raiding and interdiction of American shipping, the English commanders were expected to exact a financial price for our nation's actions against the former mother country.

In 1814, Commodore Richard Ragget of *H.M.S. Spenser* demanded a sum of $4,000 from the town of Brewster as the price to save their bayside saltworks. Fearing the power of the warship, the town of Brewster paid the amount. Ragget also shook down Eastham for $1,200. Both towns petitioned the Commonwealth for reimbursement, yet with no results.

Other towns refused to pay what amounted to thinly veiled extortion, hoping that luck and geography might save them. Orleans actually called out its militia and successfully kept British raiders from *H.M.S. Newcastle* at bay in the so-called "Battle of Rock Harbor."

Loring Crocker of Barnstable, who owned the largest complex of saltworks in that village, was able to purchase four cannons in Boston and had them transferred to the bluffs above the common fields. Perhaps it was his cannons or the fact that the British couldn't get their large vessel close enough to shore to bring his enterprise within cannon fire, but there is no record that he, or anyone else in Barnstable, paid the $6,000 demanded by the *Spenser*.

On the Cape's south side, there is historical evidence that Yarmouth tried without success to avoid payment of a $1,000 sum to Captain Charles Gollett of the frigate *H.M.S. Nymph* in July of 1814. It seems that when the frigate showed up at the entrance of Bass River looking for privateers, the townspeople decided to send one of its mentally handicapped citizens out to the vessel in a small boat. He carried the message that all of the people of South Yarmouth were like him, as well as poor and destitute, and therefore not worth a stop. The ruse, however, did not work and the warship moved into position to blast the local saltworks as the tides rose in the river. Yarmouth paid its share quickly.

During the 1976 national bicentennial, Brewster selectmen, apparently still smarting about having to pay $4,000 to the British almost 200 years earlier, sent off a letter to Queen Elizabeth II asking that the sum be returned as a gesture of good will. As of this date Brewster is still waiting for an answer. At least the British government is no different than the Massachusetts State Legislature in settling accounts quickly.

The Battle Over Missing Tackle

Orleans is one of only two Cape Cod towns attacked by the British during the War of 1812, the other being Falmouth. The events at Orleans, known as the "Battle of Rock Harbor," vary a bit from history book to history book but generally take the shape of the following. The British were demanding ransoms from Cape towns to save their saltworks from destruction. They wanted $2,000 from Orleans, who refused to pay and as a result were attacked. Orleans won the battle, though two sloops were burned in the harbor and another sloop and a schooner were seized by the British. The saltworks escaped unharmed.

Yet another tale tells that the saltworks were not really the focus of the attack. The event, which occurred just days before the signing of the Treaty of Ghent in December 1814 thus ending the war, actually took place over the course of a week, with the final day, the 19th of December, culminating in a battle.

On December 12, the British warship *H.M.S. Newcastle* grounded off Wellfleet. To lighten her load, the captain ordered her spars and rigging and other heavy tackle and equipment tossed overboard. Much of this tackle drifted southward to Orleans, collecting at Rock Harbor where it was "vandalized" by the local militia. The next day a British search crew discovered the missing tackle, yet were unable to retrieve it. They did, though, seize the American vessel *Camel*. On December 19, four British boats commanded by Lt. Frederick Marryat arrived at Rock Harbor to take back their tackle. They seized one vessel, the *Betsy*, burned two others, and after discovering that the tackle had been damaged, set fire to the saltworks and the pier. The local militia drove the British out of the harbor, killing at least one invader in the process.

The residents of Orleans then expected the *Newcastle*, with her 64 cannons, to arrive the next day to level the town, but the warship never arrived. She left Cape Cod waters in search of the *USS Constitution*, which, it was rumored, had slipped past the British blockade while the *Newcastle* was grounded.

Slavery and Cape Cod

It was probably the nature of the economy more than anything else that decided the question of slavery for Cape Cod. Without the need for labor-intensive agriculture (the cranberry industry did not start until the nineteenth century), there was never the demand for slaves on a wide scale in Massachusetts. Yet there is evidence that slavery did exist on Cape Cod as late as the early part of the nineteenth century.

As Henry Kittredge notes in his book, *Cape Cod: Its People and Their History*, "... from 1640 until well after the Revolution, slaves were common in all parts of the Old Colony, and if there were fewer on the Cape than elsewhere, it was only because there were fewer rich men or extensive landowners."

A close examination of old records makes it quite clear that a number of prominent Cape Cod families owned slaves. Plymouth Colony records note that in 1678 three Native Indians from Sandwich were convicted of breaking into the house of Zachariah Allen. They were sentenced by the court to be "perpetual slaves" to the

Allen family. In the same period, as a result of the King Philip's
War, a number of Indians were sold into slavery within the colony.
Some, including the family of King Philip himself, were sold to
places as far away as the Caribbean islands.

The Harvard-educated Reverend John Cotton, who preached in
Yarmouth in the last years of the seventeenth century, was com-
pensated with a house and an Indian slave named Saxuant.
Another Cape preacher, Deacon Thomas Parker of Falmouth, had a
slave named "Cuffee" who was declared "sufficiently white" to
worship along side of the rest of the congregation in 1732.

Shebnah Rich's *Truro - Cape Cod* mentions that the last black
slave in that town was a man named Hector who was the property
of Benjamin Collins. Hector was the son of a black slave named Joe
and an unnamed female slave owned by Jonathan Paine. In 1726,
Paine sold Hector, then three years old, to Collins for a sum of 30
English pounds. It is recorded that in 1747 the Reverend John
Avery baptized Hector in the Truro church. Hector lived as a single
man to old age in Truro off South Pamet Road and when he died
he was buried in an unmarked grave. His memory is kept alive by
a section of the town near the Pamet Highlands called variously as
"Hector's Stubble," "Hector's Bridge," "Hector's Nook," and "Old
Hector."

Another slave named Pomp, who was owned by the same
Jonathan Paine, committed suicide by hanging himself from a tree
in the woodlot of his master. The spot thereafter took the name
"Pomp's Lot."

In Joseph Paine's *History of Harwich*, there is a notation that Mrs.
Samuel Hall sold three slaves to her nephew, John Allen, in 1756.
Benjamin Bangs wrote in a December 1760 letter to a friend, "I sold
my negro Oliver and very glad to get rid of him for thirty nine
pounds of lawful money to Eleazer Nickerson of Bass Ponds and
he is gone this day; this is ye seventh master he has had; good
riddance of bad rubbish."

Another Harwich slaveholder was Zachariah Smalley. At his
death in 1779, his will stipulated that his slave "Toby" was to be
provided for by his heirs for as long as he should live. In Barnstable, John Bacon bequeathed to his wife the "use and improve-

ment" of his slave Dinah. The will stipulated that Dinah was to be
sold if she outlived her mistress and the money was to be used for
the purchase of Bibles to be distributed to members of the Bacon
family. *The History of Old Yarmouth*, by Charles Swift, cites the
purchase of a slave by Benjamin Homer with reference to a bill of
sale dated February 20, 1776.

By the time of the American Revolution, Cape Cod, along with
the rest of Massachusetts, was ready to legislate the end to slavery.
Sandwich town records note that at the May 18, 1773 town meeting
voters instructed the town's representative to the General Court
"to endeavor to have an Act passed by the Court, to prevent the
importation of slaves into this country, and that all children that
shall be born of such Africans as are now slaves among us shall,
after such Act, be free at 21 years of age."

Perhaps the last living person on Cape Cod who could claim to
have started life as a slave was Robert Claybrook. He was a slave
in South Carolina when the Civil War gave him the opportunity to
travel to Massachusetts. Claybrook settled in Bournedale in the
vicinity of Herring Pond and lived into the early part of the
twentieth century.

Another connection to the age of slavery was George Thomas
Washington. Born the son of a slave, Washington arrived on Cape
Cod in 1868 and settled in Hyannis where he became a successful
farmer. He died at the age of 104 in 1958.

The Man with the Branded Hand

As a coasting captain in the 1830s, Jonathan Walker of East
Harwich made a number of voyages to southern ports. There he
saw, first hand, the evils of the so-called "peculiar institution."

He became an early convert to the growing abolitionist movement that was beginning to play on the consciences of a number of
Americans. Apparently a literate man, Walker wrote at least a few
early anti-slavery pieces. He stated that slavery "ranked with the
highest wrongs and crimes that ever were invented by the enemy
of man." And he declared that the keeping of human slaves was
equivalent to "family, community, political and national poison."

In 1844, Captain Walker attempted to smuggle several slaves to Nassau from the port of Pensacola, Florida. It was not the first time that he had done this. As his ship left Florida, however, it was intercepted by a state patrol vessel near Key West and his cargo of human contraband discovered. Walker was arrested and taken back to Pensacola and imprisoned while awaiting trial.

With the assistance of the abolitionist press, Captain Walker's predicament became known in the northern region of the nation. His detention was something of a *cause celébre* in anti-slavery circles and a number of rallies were held in New York and Boston to demand his freedom. When he finally did come to trial in Pensacola after months of detention he was convicted of slave stealing and his penalty was to be branded on the right hand with the letters "S.S." for "slave stealer."

The cruelty of this degrading punishment stirred intense anger in the north. In the view of the radical northern press, there was nothing more inhuman than to brand another human being. The news of the Captain's sentence aroused masses of protest in the north and when he returned in June of 1845 to New York City, Walker was received as a hero. Speaking in Lynn, Massachusetts a month later he said, "I repent not of what I have done. As long as life remains in me, this hand and this voice shall be raised against slavery that shameful violation of all the rights of man and all the laws of God."

He appeared on the anti-slavery circuit for several years with some of the leading abolitionists of the pre-Civil War period, including Wendell Phillips, Theodore Parker, Stephen S. Foster, Parker Pillsbury, and Charles Sumner. At rallies his main purpose was to warm up the crowds by showing his branded hand, which would drive the audience into a frenzy of anger toward all slaveholders.

Never a wealthy man, Captain Walker's fortunes waned to the point that he was near poverty by the early 1850s. He was rarely paid as a lecturer and he was barely able to support his family by selling anti-slavery pamphlets. In 1853, Walker moved his family to Sheboygan County, Wisconsin and began a new life of farming. There he lived in relative obscurity, but still wrote occasional pieces for anti-slavery publications.

When the Civil War came he volunteered his services for the Freedman's Bureau in Washington, but he was ignored. Returning again to the west and Muskegon County, Michigan, he operated a small farm until his death on April 30, 1873 at the age of seventy-four. He was buried by neighbors who were unaware of his story and his early role in the abolition movement. When news of his death reached Boston, a number of former abolitionists raised a sum of money for a 10-foot high monument to the man with the branded hand. The marker is still in the city of Muskegon and features the lines of a poem by John Greenleaf Whittier:

"Then lift that manly right hand
Bold ploughman of the wave;
Its branded palm shall prophesy
Salvation to the slave.

Hold up its fire-wrought language
That whoso reads may feel
His heart swell strong within him,
His sinews changed to steel."

Cape Cod's Civil War General

The Civil War saw many Cape Cod volunteers for the Army and Navy. Scores of young men enlisted in the cause and many distinguished themselves on various battlefields during the conflict. Only one Cape-born man, though, rose to the military rank of General and that man was Joseph Eldridge Hamblin of Yarmouth.

Despite the common puffery and inflated exploits that often surfaced when tales of wartime service were recounted by later generations, it does appear that General Hamblin was a real battlefield leader and not simply one of the political appointee military bureaucrats of which the war produced so many. Born to Benjamin and Hannah Hamblin on January 13, 1828, young Joe Hamblin spent his youthful days between Cape Cod and Boston. He also spent time at sea aboard a clipper ship commanded by Joshua Sears and traveled to China.

In 1854, he moved to New York and entered the insurance business. While in that city, he joined the 7th Regiment of the New York State National Guard. When the war broke out in 1861, Hamblin was mustered in as a First Lieutenant and saw his first battle action in June of 1861 at Big Bethel. Continuing in the field, Hamblin was promoted successively to Captain, Major, and later to Lieutenant Colonel in not much more than a year. In July of 1862, he gained the rank of full Colonel and took part in the subsequent battles of Fredericksburg, Chancellorsville, and the

Yarmouth's Civil War General Joseph Eldridge Hamblin, who saw combat from 1861 to 1865 and died of battle-related wounds in 1870. (William Brewster Nickerson Room Collection - Cape Cod Community College)

decisive Union victory at Gettysburg.

In the spring of 1864, Colonel Hamblin served under Ulysses Grant in the Wilderness Campaign and later went into the Shenandoah Valley Campaign with General Horatio Wright, fighting in the battles of Winchester, Fisher's Hill, and Cedar Creek. In the October Cedar Creek battle, while serving under General Phil Sheridan, Hamblin was given command of a brigade. He was severely wounded in his right leg while holding a line of retreat for Union forces. His efforts contributed to the Federal victory there. On the recommendation of General Sheridan, he received a field promotion to Brigadier General for "gallant and meritorious services."

After a brief recuperation period, General Hamblin returned to the struggle and participated in all of the engagements of the Army of the Potomac to the final Confederate surrender at Appomattox, Virginia. In one of the last engagements of the war, he was wounded again at Sayler's Creek and received another field promotion to Major General for "conspicuous gallantry." He left the service at the war's end with that rank, the highest of any Cape Cod man in the struggle. During the entire war he took only one 10-day leave of absence and was actively involved in the major campaigns with the exception of a three-month home leave while convalescing from his wounds.

Sadly, he was not to live a long and happy post-war life. Only five years after the end of the war, he died on July 3, 1870 from service-related injuries. His grave is in the Summer Street cemetery in Yarmouthport. As one historian and contemporary wrote, "He was instinctively looked upon as a leader of men, being of fine and commanding person, and of noble presence. His social qualities and chivalrous disposition endeared him to those with whom he came in familiar contact."

Captain Levi Crowell - Civil War Prisoner

Captain Levi Crowell, Jr. of West Dennis was born in October 1827. He was the great-great-great-great-great grandson of John Crow who, along with Thomas Howes, first settled the lands now known as Dennis.

At the age of 18, young Levi Crowell first went to sea as a cook on board the schooner *Boston*. He rose up through the ranks to captain over the following 15 years until 1860 and the coming of the Civil War. In December 1861, he received orders from the U.S. Navy to accept an Acting Master position. By the end of the year he reported for service aboard the steamer *Sumter*.

In May 1862, while off Georgia, Crowell commanded a cutter with orders to pilot the vessel up a creek to Fort Pulaski. He never reached his intended destination. The 13th Georgia Regiment captured Crowell's vessel and crew and the Union soldiers became prisoners of war. Crowell kept a diary while in prison, which has since been reprinted in the book *History of Levi Crowell*. On June 19 he wrote: *"Our fate is miserable. We do not have more than enough to eat. I go hungry."* July 10 has this entry: *"Every morning we all examine our clothing and hunt for lice. My bedfellow this morning found four and I found one on the sheets."*

Crowell and his crew were taken to a prison in Atlanta until the end of June and then transferred to another prison in Madison, Georgia until his release during a prisoner exchange in October after nearly five months of imprisonment. His October 7th entry reads: *"And one long to be remembered by us all as the day we left our Rebel prison and took our departure for the North, bound home. How my heart beats when I write that word: home."*

Losing a great deal of weight during his incarceration, Crowell went home to West Dennis to recuperate before rejoining the Union ranks in January 1863, serving on the steamer *Union* for the duration of the war. After retiring from the sea in the 1880s, Levi Crowell lived to nearly the age of 90, expiring in 1917 while Cape Cod boys were away fighting in another Great War.

The Mutual Support Club

While most popular histories of the Civil War paint a picture of Cape Cod patriotism and heroic deeds, there was another side to the conflict and that was avoidance of conscription.

In Truro, a group of over 100 draft eligible men joined an association known as the Mutual Support Club whose mission was to pool money to purchase a soldier-substitute who would then serve in a member's place. Shebnah Rich, in his book *Truro Landmarks and Seamarks*, recorded the charter of the club as follows: "We the subscribers, each agree to pay the sum of twenty-five dollars toward a fund for furnishing three hundred dollars to such members of the club as are drafted to the war. If the Club does not subscribe sufficient money to pay three hundred dollars to each and every member drafted, then it shall be applied in proportion to the amount subscribed. N.B. Should any member of this Club drafted not be accepted by Government, he shall refund the money advanced, for the benefit of the Club." Signed at Truro, May 16, 1864.

There is evidence that after the war, the members of the Club, none of whom were ever called to serve, collected their original investment with interest.

Fort "Useless"

Cape Cod, because of its exposed geographical position, has always suffered from the possibility of enemy attack from the sea. Indeed, during both the Revolutionary War and the War of 1812 the peninsula was temporarily blockaded and occupied by enemy forces.

Cape Codders were conscious of this vulnerability and during the Civil War they petitioned the U.S. Government to build a fort that would protect Provincetown from an attack by Confederate naval forces. Actually, the fear was not that unfounded. Confederate sea raiders like the *C.S.S. Alabama* had attacked and sunk a number of ships from the New England whaling fleets. In several cases, Cape Cod skippers had been menaced by these vessels. Captain Benjamin Howes of Dennis lost his clipper *Southern Cross* in 1863 to the Confederate warship *Florida*. Eastham's Captain Edward Penniman barely escaped being sunk by the *C.S.S. Shenandoah* while whaling in the bark *Minerva*.

Provincetown, with the largest fleet of ships and the most exposed piece of geography on Cape Cod, naturally felt it should be protected. After much wrangling, the Federal Government did put up two small fortifications on Long Point. There were a couple of cannons placed at strategic angles and some soldiers mustered to man the trenches. The forts were placed under the command of Sgt. Major John Rosenthall, who was later the town tax collector. Rosenthall's son, Irving, would become Provincetown's principal photographer by the beginning of the twentieth century.

By the time the war ended in 1865, the forts became the subject of ridicule by most residents. There seemed to be a sort of Gilbert and Sullivan atmosphere around the defenses as residents picnicked in the shade of the guns and critics began to refer to them as "Fort Useless" and "Fort Harmless." One historian called one of the bulwarks "Fort Ridiculous."

At no time was a shot ever fired in anger from either of the structures and gradually they were abandoned in 1872 to the shifting sand of Long Point. Today, there is nothing but two small hillocks to mark the spot where men in blue kept a sharp eye out for rebel invaders that, thankfully, never came.

Chapter 9

The Lost Dauphin &
Other Cape Cod Visitors

Cape Cod has always attracted people to its shores. Princes, premiers, prisoners, pilgrims, performers, and presidents have all walked the landscape of the Cape, their shadows remaining behind for decades and centuries after their departure.

Some of those who arrived remained for just a short time, yet their presence, however brief, has become part of the peninsula's long and storied history. Cape Cod has served as a stopping over point for wandering souls, from a band of Vikings that supposedly landed a millennium ago, to naturalist writers that sought understanding amongst the dunes, right on up to modern day visitors who arrive with suitcase in hand to enjoy a vacation of sea and sun and sand. All were impressed by Cape Cod, and in return left their impression on the Cape for years and generations to follow.

Many others arrived not for a visit, but for a lifetime, making the peninsula their home. As each new group made its presence felt on the peninsula the character and culture of Cape Cod changed.

Sometimes the settling in process had some rough edges, but like the richness of a slowly simmering soup, the texture and fabric of Cape Cod life took on its own unique flavor with the arrival of new people and new ideas.

The composite experiences of these many "wash-ashores," and their contributions to what Cape Cod has eventually become, is a wonderful part of our history. In this chapter we will feature just a few of these characters who had no deep roots in the sands of Cape Cod, but who are part and parcel of the chronicle of this narrow land.

Early Visitors to Nauset

Nauset Beach has long attracted visitors to its beautiful coastline, visitors drawn from both near and faraway places. Most of today's visitors travel to Nauset by automobile from the mainland, but those who visited in centuries past arrived by oceangoing vessels after long, arduous voyages.

The first to arrive, roughly 1,000 years ago, was Leif Erickson and his band of Viking explorers from Iceland. The Norse sagas tell that Erickson journeyed southwest from Iceland, passing Greenland, Newfoundland, and Nova Scotia to arrive along Cape Cod's eastern shore. The tales mention that he made landfall at an ancient island off the coast of Nauset Beach. He and his crew named the place "Wonderstrand" before sailing around Monomoy Island and into Nantucket Sound.

Though it is pretty much accepted that Basque fishermen, and perhaps even the Celts, visited the waters off Cape Cod in the centuries following the Viking's arrival, the next person of note to arrive at Nauset was English explorer Bartholomew Gosnold who anchored off the beach in 1602. His journey of discovery around the peninsula resulted in the naming of many landmarks, including Cape Cod itself, Martha's Vineyard, and the Elizabeth Islands.

The year 1605 saw the arrival of French explorer Samuel de Champlain at Nauset Harbor. Champlain made contact with the Nauset Indians and at first it appeared that the two groups were making some headway toward friendly relations. Unfortunately, those relations turned sour over what was perhaps a simple misunderstanding. The French accused one of the Indians of stealing a copper pot. During a skirmish, one French sailor was killed. Champlain and his men departed, returning to Chatham the next year to do further battle with the Monomoyick Indians.

Explorer Henry Hudson claimed to have sighted a mermaid off Nauset Beach in 1609. Captains John Smith and Thomas Hunt sailed past the area in 1614, as did the Pilgrims in 1620 before reaching Provincetown Harbor. It would not be until 1644 that settlement of Nauset would occur and not until the turn of the eighteenth century that settlement at Orleans, then known as Pochet, finally took root.

Brewster and the Lost Dauphin

The town of Brewster had, as part of its lore, the story of how Captain David Nickerson reportedly rescued the son of King Louis XVI of France and brought the heir to the Bourbon throne to Cape Cod.

Popular histories recounted the tale that during the French Revolution, in the confusion of the Reign of Terror, Captain Nickerson was in Paris awaiting clearance to sail when a woman ran up to him and thrust a small baby into his arms. It was, she told him, the son of Louis XVI who she claimed had been rescued and spirited away from imprisonment by loyalists. She begged Nickerson to take the child to America where he would be safe.

Good Captain Nickerson did as he was bid and returned to Brewster where he raised the child as his own. The story has it that the boy was given the name Rene Rousseau, undoubtedly in honor of his French roots. He reportedly followed the calling of the sea as most Cape Cod boys did in the nineteenth century. By age 20 he was an expert seaman and a few years later he was master of his own ship. But the young man's luck ran out at age 25 when he was lost at sea. Captain Nickerson survived his adopted son for five years before dying of fever during a voyage to Africa aboard the ship *Ten Brothers* in 1819.

This would normally be the end of this interesting story. Versions

of what happened to the young son of the deposed French mon-
arch can be found throughout Europe and America. But Brewster
goes a step further with its claim by always citing a weathered
gravestone located in the ancient burial ground behind the First
Parish Church where the names of Captain David Nickerson and
Rene Rousseau were carved together. That was proof enough of
Brewster's connection to the so-called Lost Dauphin.

Modern science has always challenged myths and legends. Such is
the case with this tale. A news story was published during 2000
stating that university researchers, performing DNA tests comparing the preserved heart of a 10-year old boy with hair from the
remains of Queen Marie Antoinette, conclusively proved that the
child was her son, Louis XVII, the Lost Dauphin. A doctor had
stolen the heart while performing an autopsy on a young royal
prisoner in 1795. It was preserved and hidden for many years before
it ended up in a crystal vase in the royal crypt outside of Paris.
According to the researchers, the scientific tests are indisputable.

But one tends to become a skeptic about most things, even when
scientists put their imprimatur on them. In a town of solid English
origins, why would a local captain name his son after a French
enlightenment writer? Nickerson was reportedly in Paris during
the chaos of the Revolution. Might not someone have switched the
king's child with another baby and spirited it off to safety?

The stone, though difficult to read, was still in the cemetery as
late as the 1970s, but was removed for safekeeping by the church.
Legend and myth are part of the richness of history, and the story
of Captain Nickerson and the Lost Dauphin will always be part of
Brewster's past.

Thoreau's 1849 Visit to Orleans

In October 1849, during his first visit to Cape Cod, naturalist
writer Henry David Thoreau journeyed briefly through Orleans as
documented in his book, *Cape Cod*.

After spending a foggy evening at Higgins Tavern he trudged
through a rainy Cape Cod day, happening upon shell heaps and an
ancient boat canal as he traveled north toward Eastham. "Every

landscape which is dreary enough has a certain beauty to my eyes, and in this instance its permanent qualities were enhanced by the weather," said Thoreau of Orleans in the rain. The naturalist then made observations on the economy of the area, stating that "the shores are more fertile than the dry land" and "the inhabitants measure their crops, not only by bushels of corn, but by barrels of clams." He mentioned that there were "heaps of shells in the fields, where clams had been opened for bait; for Orleans is known for its shell-fish, especially clams." Of the clam supply, Thoreau concluded that it was "inexhaustible."

Just before leaving Orleans and entering Eastham, Thoreau commented on the creek that flows between the two towns, which during much of the eighteenth century and the first decades of the nineteenth century was a boat canal known as Jeremiah's Gutter. "We crossed a brook, not more than fourteen rods long between Orleans and Eastham ... The Atlantic is said sometimes to meet the Bay here, and isolate the northern part of the Cape." Naturalist writer Henry Beston, who wrote the classic book *The Outermost House* and the introduction to the 1951 edition of Thoreau's *Cape Cod*, offered the following footnote: "Eighteenth-century maps show this 'gutter' as a small-boat channel connecting Orleans Cove with the bay. It has long since disappeared but a folk memory of its existence lingers on the Cape."

Thoreau returned to Orleans in June 1857, and again visited the gutter, writing, "Jeremiah's Gutter is what is called Boat Meadow River on the map ... was somebody's Folly, who dug a canal, which the sand filled up again."

Thoreau's 1857 Visit to Yarmouth

Henry David Thoreau made four journeys to this narrow land - in 1849, 1850, 1855, and 1857 - penning his observations as he went along. His 1857 journal entries were not included in *Cape Cod*, the text of the book being largely completed before his fourth and final trip. Yet, it was during this 1857 excursion that he visited Yarmouth, and his observations, though brief, are interesting. At the time he was a month shy of his 40th birthday. Within five years he would be dead.

Thoreau arrived at the north side of the town of Yarmouth on
June 16. He had earlier that day started out from Sandwich, taking
the new railroad to Yarmouthport as evidenced by his words:
"About 11 a.m. take the cars from Scusset to Sandwich. See in the
marshes by the railroad the *Potentilla anserina* ..." Upon arriving at
Yarmouthport he asked at the ticket office for directions to Friends
Village in the southern part of town. The man in the ticket booth
claimed to have never heard of the village.

Another man, "a stage-driver" remarked that the village was
five miles away and then directed Thoreau to first walk the entire
length of Main Street along his way to his destination. This both-
ered Thoreau, feeling that he was being sent the long way around,
and after a while "I turned off earlier than they directed, and
found that, as usual, I might have taken a shorter route across the
fields and avoided the town altogether." He further wrote, "I have
found the compass and chart safer guides than the inhabitants."

Along his way southward he crossed hills and woodlands,
passing Long Pond before arriving at Friends Village. He mentions
nothing of the village itself, stating only "Passed through the latter
and crossed Bass River by a toll-bridge." Upon arrival at West
Harwich later in the day he made certain to mention that he was
now "some eight miles from Yarmouth Depot" where the ticket-
master on duty there had never heard of Friends Village in the
very same town.

A Trip on the River Queen

The first presidential visit to Cape Cod was made by Ulysses S.
Grant, who arrived in Hyannis from the island of Nantucket by
ferry, after which he boarded the newly completed Old Colony
Railroad for his trip to Provincetown.

President Grant's visit took place in the summer of 1874. In what
was little more than an overnight whistle-stop event, the Civil War
hero and eighteenth President addressed small crowds at local
train depots as he passed through the lower Cape villages on the
way to the Cape tip. What is not generally known is that Grant's

short visit reunited him with a piece of Civil War history.

Nine years earlier, in March of 1865, President Abraham Lincoln had met Grant aboard the paddlewheel steamer *River Queen* on the James River near Richmond. The Civil War was in its final stages and General Grant had been summoned to meet the President to discuss a closing strategy for the struggle. The Union command leadership aboard the steamer was represented by Grant, Admiral David Porter, and General William Sherman.

The *River Queen* served as Lincoln's floating headquarters for several weeks and Grant used the vessel as a dispatch boat. While engaged in a discussion about how the war should be ended, the group learned that Petersburg had fallen to Union forces and that Richmond was about to capitulate. Lincoln went to sleep aboard the *River Queen* knowing that the long struggle was about to end. Within a day the Confederate capital surrendered and the President took the news with relief and thanksgiving, eventually meeting Grant in the ruins of the rebel city. The *River Queen* was the scene of some of the most important final decisions about the war made by the President and his victorious commander.

In the years following the war, the *River Queen* was sold several times. She was operated for a time between Providence and Newport, Rhode Island and for a time ran as the sister to the steamer *Island Home* with service to Martha's Vineyard. Eventually she became the property of the Nantucket and Cape Cod Steamboat Company. At the time of Grant's visit to Cape Cod the vessel was nine years old and running between Hyannis and Nantucket. Grant recognized the former presidential command ship and made it a point to use it to connect to Hyannis.

Witnesses noted that during the short passage Grant "walked alone on the promenade deck, chewing on a cigar. For a long time he kept to himself, deep in thought. History had come to another full circle." One can only imagine Grant's feelings when he reviewed the events of history that occurred aboard the *River Queen*. The ghosts of the great Civil War figures were certainly passengers on the small steamer that day as it made its way across Nantucket Sound.

In 1892, the *River Queen* returned south after being purchased by the Mount Vernon & Marshall Hall Steamboat Company of

Washington D. C. She was still in service into the 1920s on the Potomac River as a sightseeing boat.

Helen Keller and Brewster

It is not generally known that Helen Keller spent several summers vacationing in the town of Brewster.

She was new to the New England area, having arrived in 1888 from her native Alabama at age eight with her teacher Annie Sullivan. As a young girl she sometimes stayed for part of the summer in the house at the corner of routes 124 and 6A that was owned by Captain Nathan F. Foster. At other times she stayed at another house on Main Street, which is presently called "Red Jacket Antiques." As a member of the Swedenborgian Church, there is a good chance that she attended services in nearby Yarmouthport, as it was the only local church of this denomination.

She is said to have enjoyed the swimming at Breakwater Beach. On one occasion she tried to take a horseshoe crab back to where she and Miss Sullivan were staying. She was fascinated by the feel and power of the ocean. In her eagerness to experience the sea she found herself knocked off her feet by the waves. "I thrust out my hands to grab some support, I clutched at the water and at the seaweed which the waves tossed in my face." she wrote in her autobiography. "But all my frantic efforts were in vain. The waves seemed to be playing a game with me and tossed me from one to another in their wild frolic. It was fearful! The good, firm earth had slipped from my feet, and everything seemed shut out from this strange all-enveloping element - life, air, warmth, and love. At last, however, the sea, as if weary of its new toy, threw me back on the shore, and in another instant I was clasped in my teacher's arms ... As soon as I had recovered from my panic sufficiently to say anything, I demanded, 'Who put salt in the water?'"

Grover Cleveland's Cape Cod Secret

We live in an age that gives us instant media coverage of just about everything. To imagine the whereabouts of the President of the United States unknown for even a few moments in the day is almost unthinkable. Even more unthinkable is the notion that secrets can be kept by government officials in the face of intense media scrutiny, especially as they relate to the president's health and whereabouts.

But a century ago it was possible for the Chief Executive of the country to lead an almost normal life when away from official duties in Washington. While on vacation, presidents certainly were of some interest to local people, but there seemed to be an attitude in that time that they were entitled to their privacy. One of the things that President Grover Cleveland enjoyed most about living at his summer home on Cape Cod was the fact that the citizens of Bourne left him pretty much alone. "My neighbors are independent, not obtrusively curious, and I have only to behave myself and pay my taxes to be treated like any other citizen of the United States," he told a visitor to his summer home at Gray Gables. He generally spent his summer months away from Washington living as a gentleman farmer and fisherman while relaxing on the shores of Buzzards Bay.

The summer White House – President Grover Cleveland's Gray Gables at Bourne. (J. Coogan collection)

Thus, there appeared to be nothing unusual when on June 30, 1893, Cleveland, now in the first year of his second term as President, left Washington for his Cape Cod home. Most of the government had suspended operations anyway and Congress was not in session. The President's wife was already in Bourne and he was scheduled to join her for six weeks of vacation. Cleveland boarded a train and headed for New York City where he was to travel by steam yacht to Cape Cod.

But in fact, there was something very unusual going on during this trip to Cape Cod and the President and his closest advisors didn't want anyone to know about it. Only two weeks earlier, Cleveland had been examined by his personal physician, Dr. Robert O'Reilly, after complaining of a sore mouth. The examination revealed that the President had a malignancy that had to be removed. Cleveland had no hesitation about the operation, but he did not want to panic the nation by revealing his cancer. Calling in his inner circle, the decision was made to have the operation at sea while the President and his party sailed up Long Island Sound to Gray Gables.

Cleveland, accompanied by his friend and personal physician, Dr. Joseph Bryant, boarded Commodore Elias C. Benedict's steam

---

NO SIGN OF THE ONEIDA.

The President Has Not Yet Arrived at Gray Gables.

BUZZARD'S BAY, Mass., July 3.—The weather is thick in Buzzard's Bay, and there are no signs of the yacht Oneida, having on board the Presidential party. Nothing has been heard of the party since they left New-York.

The yacht left New-York Friday night. The usual run is fifteen hours, and inasmuch as the boat has not been reported at any of the ports, it is the opinion here that the yacht is at anchor down the bay awaiting the clearing of the thick fog, which will allow her to proceed.

Article that appeared in the New York Times on July 4, 1893 questioning the whereabouts of President Cleveland.

yacht *Oneida* for what was ostensibly to be a leisurely cruise to his summer home. The *Oneida* had been fitted out secretly with a state of the art operating room. A special chair had been set up to hold the portly President in position for the delicate operation. Dentist William Keen of Philadelphia was to perform the oral surgery with Dr. Bryant removing the cancer. The operation was a difficult one because the President would be under heavy ether and there was the possibility that he could accidentally choke to death. A heavy man, Cleveland could potentially go into a cardiac shock if he choked.

On the morning of July 1, not long after departing the East River, the operation began. After almost two hours of cutting and scraping, the fairly large cancerous mass was removed and the cavity packed. Great care was taken to contain the work to the inside of the mouth so as to leave no visible scar. The President was given some morphine and put to bed where he slept for almost 24 hours.

By this time the *Oneida* had been at sea for two days. Normally the trip across the sound to Gray Gables was an overnight passage, never much more than 15 to 20 hours. The yacht stayed at sea on July 3 without contacting any other vessels. Reporters who arrived at Buzzards Bay on July 2 began to show concern for the missing President. The *New York Times* ran a story on July 4th headlined, "No Sign of the *Oneida*." Fog was attributed to the delay of the yacht.

On the afternoon of July 4th, the *Oneida* stopped briefly at Sag Harbor on Long Island to put one of the assisting doctors ashore. The President called his wife at Gray Gables and she briefed the press as to the safety of her husband. She made no mention of the operation although she knew about it. Secrecy was to be maintained at all costs.

Late on July 5th the *Oneida* moored in Buzzards Bay and the President walked under his own power up the gangway to his home. It was all for show because Cleveland was still suffering from the effects of the operation and headed immediately to bed. Some reporters were suspicious. Why had the President taken so long to get to Buzzards Bay? Was he seriously ill? What was not being said?

Cleveland's spokesman, Dan Lamont, told reporters that the President was suffering from rheumatism and that he had had several bad teeth pulled during the trip up the sound. Most everyone bought the story. Several days later Cleveland was able to go on a very public fishing trip with friends and rumors died down. About two weeks later, he went aboard the *Oneida* again for a short overnight cruise during which some additional surgery was secretly accomplished.

For the remainder of July, President Cleveland recovered at Gray Gables. He was well enough to return to Washington in August for the opening of Congress. No one ever knew the real story of the slow trip across Long Island Sound.

Cleveland died in 1908, not of cancer but of heart disease. Unbelievably, the truth of the *Oneida's* role in the cancer operation and the very real danger to the life of the President of the United States was not revealed until 1917, long after all the parties were dead.

"Tiger of Vendee" at Yarmouth

It was the summer of 1867. The Civil War was over and the citizens of Cape Cod were returning to their pre-war pursuits of farming and fishing.

In South Yarmouth a young Frenchman was a guest at the Main Street home of Miss Catherine Aiken. His connection to Miss Aiken stemmed from his duties as a language teacher in her Stamford, Connecticut Female Seminary and he was making his first visit to Cape Cod. As a vocal political opponent of the regime of Napoleon III, he was also temporarily in exile in the United States. The young man was George Clemenceau, the man who would eventually become Premier of France and one of the great figures of World War I.

All of this, however, was far in the future during that summer of 1867 as the young teacher relaxed between semesters along the shores of Bass River. Clemenceau was quick to see that there was much more to a Cape Cod summer than fishing and sailing on the river and he began to keep steady company with one of Miss Aiken's visiting female students, 18-year old Mary Plummer of New York.

People who met the young Frenchman remembered him as "an enjoyable companion," and praised his extensive knowledge of world affairs. His presence was a charming attraction to the ordinary life of this quiet village. He seems clearly, however, to have been involved in another kind of affair with Miss Plummer because two years later, in 1869, the future "Tiger of Vendee" married her in New York's City Hall without the consent of her guardians.

Prisoners of War

In present time when there has been considerable hue and cry about the placement of the County Jail on the grounds of the former Camp Edwards in Bourne, it seems interesting that 50 years earlier prisoners were accepted and even made welcome at the same facility. These were not the everyday criminal types that make their way through the present judicial system. They were German prisoners of World War II who were under guard by American military police.

Officially, the Camp Edwards facility was named the East Coast Processing Center and prisoners were assigned temporary placement before being shipped to more secure facilities, usually inland. When the center opened in 1943 it was intended as a holding area for American military personnel who were guilty of infractions such as desertion or chronic cases of "missing movement." Several thousand of these men ended up at Edwards. Here they were court-martialed and awarded various sentences. The capacity of the stockade was 3,000, though rarely was this number reached.

The first instance of German prisoners arriving at Camp Edwards took place in April of 1943 when the Nazis were driven out of North Africa. These were mostly members of Rommel's Africa Corps. Other German POWs began to arrive in the summer of 1944. Many of these were captured in the days following the Normandy invasion of France in early June.

Most of the prisoners' days at Edwards were spent in general base maintenance. But there were also instances where prisoners were allowed out to pick cranberries or strawberries as contract laborers. Some of them worked regularly in the quartermaster laundry in Falmouth on King Street. Perhaps the most important work that was done outside of the base was the clean up that took place after the severe fall hurricane of 1944. Working with four portable saw mills, the prisoners salvaged eight million feet of lumber around Cape Cod.

Despite the feelings connected with the war, most Cape Codders looked at the prisoners not so much as hated enemies, but more as poor young unfortunates that had been caught up in something over which they had little control. Seeing the young and handsome prisoners was an occasion for not just a few local women to consider the idea of literally "loving one's enemy." One teenager and her friends, while passing the work details in an open-roofed Model A Ford, waved so vigorously that the guard pulled them over and reminded them that these were not the boys from next door.

Occasionally one of the Germans would attempt escape. On October 14, 1944, a prisoner ran away from a work detail in Cotuit. His name was Victor Gleiberger. The approaches to the Cape Cod Canal were closed and vehicles searched. Gleiberger, who spoke no English and whose presence could not help but attract attention in a community where most young men were overseas, had little chance of evading capture. He was caught after a few days and nights of hiding in the woods and bogs of Santuit. His attempt at freedom was an exception to the well-ordered group of prisoners that were housed at Camp Edwards.

At the war's end in the spring of 1945 the POWs were repatriated. An estimated 5,000 prisoners had passed through the facility. Their experience on Cape Cod completed, they returned home to rebuild their lives.

The Song That Made Cape Cod Famous

When singer Patti Page showed up to perform at the Cape Cod Melody Tent in August of 1977, many Cape Codders embraced her as the person who really put Cape Cod on the map. It was the occasion of the twentieth anniversary of her hit song *"Old Cape Cod,"* a tune that soared to prominence just before the John F. Kennedy presidential years and the family mystique that made the peninsula a national tourist destination.

Originally expected to be the secondary side of the Mercury label record that also featured the tune *"I'm Wondering,"* the song was written by a housewife and dentist from the Boston area. Claire Rothrock provided the words along with Milt Yakus, and Allan Jeffrey wrote the music. It was the only hit tune that the group ever wrote and it immortalized the traditional image of Cape Cod.

Miss Page was an unlikely booster of the Cape. She was from Oklahoma and hadn't spent a great deal of time near the ocean. She did have a hit record in the 1950s about Tennessee, that being the *"The Tennessee Waltz."* She recorded *"Old Cape Cod"* before she had ever visited the peninsula and she later admitted that she knew absolutely nothing about the place.

The New Pilgrims

On July 21, 1948, a storm-tossed vessel that was low on fuel and food made its way into Provincetown Harbor. The 64-foot ketch *Gundel*, with 15 men, seven women, and seven children aboard dropped anchor just after noon at the western end of the harbor.

Her crew then waited for something to happen. The passengers had no papers, few possessions, and no homes. Their vessel had been 43 days at sea from Dover, England on a voyage that in many ways paralleled the course and mission of the *Mayflower* in 1620.

The *Gundel's* passengers were Latvian refugees who fled the Baltic region during World War II to escape Nazi and Russian tyranny. They originally made their way to neutral Sweden in 1944 as Russian troops occupied Latvia. While Sweden offered temporary safety in the immediate years after the war, there was talk that all Latvians would be deported back to the Soviet occupied Baltic States. This effectively meant exile to Siberia. The *Gundel's* passengers worked at their trades and crafts for several years to purchase a vessel that would take them to freedom. After pooling their money to obtain the ship, the families took the *Gundel* to England where, as displaced persons, they were denied permanent residency. Undaunted, they made up their minds to sail west to America.

With just a worn chart of the Atlantic Ocean, a stopwatch, and an old sextant, the *Gundel's* captain successfully navigated the Atlantic and made landfall at the Cape tip. Without papers, the Coast Guard immediately quarantined them as illegal immigrants. When it was learned that the people on the *Gundel* were refugees and in need of food, the citizens of Provincetown took matters into their own hands, ignoring the quarantine, and soon cases of food were going to the people on board. The local Red Cross organized supplies for the weary refugees. These included bread, milk, sugar, coffee, tea, flour, and meat. There were tears of joy among the Latvians at the generous reception given to them by the Cape tip.

Because Provincetown was not a certified American port of entry, the *Gundel* was directed to sail to Boston under Coast Guard escort. The voyage to Boston took place on July 22 after about a 30-hour stay in Provincetown Harbor.

When it was later learned that authorities might force the passengers on the *Gundel* to return to Europe, there was a loud protest throughout New England. In Provincetown, residents pointed out that these unfortunate souls were almost a mirror image of the original Pilgrims who left Europe over 300 years earlier for freedom in America. They noted that the *Gundel* itself was actually about 25 feet shorter than the *Mayflower*. In much the same way that the Pilgrims had made their famous compact, the Latvians had taken an oath while anchored at Provincetown to "live in peace, away from the Iron Curtain, seeking a chance for honest labor ... where we could earn our honest living and be free from fears."

During these first years of the Cold War there was a good deal of sympathy for the plight of these new Pilgrims. After their trip across Massachusetts Bay to East Boston, the passengers were detained by immigration officials. Over the winter many people made efforts on their behalf. Senator Henry Cabot Lodge and U.S. Representative John F. Kennedy introduced bills in Congress to make a special exemption for the refugees. Local newspapers editorialized in their favor.

In April of 1949, the passengers of the *Gundel* were finally allowed to leave the vessel after a bond of $500 was posted for each family. They eventually were sponsored by a number of groups around New England and were able to make their homes, as had the original Pilgrims, in the peace and security of America.

Chapter
10

Built on Cape Cod

Cape Cod architecture reflects much about the people who have inhabited the narrow land. Houses are cultural artifacts that can show how people adapted their needs for shelter to the prevailing social and economic conditions of their times. Ranging from the very practical salt box and Cape Cod style homes to the flamboyant and foreign influenced Italianate and French Empire style dwellings, Cape Codders have always put their stamp of individuality on the homes that they built.

Often, when they would move to a new location, Cape Codders would take their houses with them. This process, which involved dismantling the structures and hauling them on rollers to a new site, was called "flaking."

There are many examples of houses that traveled with their owners. The Josiah Dennis Manse, for example, actually combines two houses into one. The first part of the home, which was built on the present site in the mid 1730s, was later joined by an earlier structure that had started life further west on Whig Street. This section was moved and attached to the original building sometime after 1735. It is still possible to see the uneven front window level where the two structures were joined.

Some dwellings arrived by water. Several houses in South Yarmouth were floated across the sound from Nantucket on barges. A house in Cotuit that was once owned by Charles Bearse began as a residence on Nantucket in 1840. In 1859, the structure, which is more commonly known today as the Captain Lewis Phinney house, was barged to Cotuit where it sits on Main Street.

Today, Cape Codders still do a lot of moving, but they seem pretty content now to just sell their homes rather than packing them off with them.

Historic Buildings Still Playing a Role Today

Along nearly any of Cape Cod's main routes, or even some of her lesser-traveled roads, can be found a treasure trove of old buildings, many of them two and even three centuries old.

These structures are antiquities in the form of wood and stone. They are cultural artifacts that reveal much about the people who once lived in them. Outside, their shingled edifices are temples to another time. Inside, their rooms of sloping floorboards are filled with relics, century-old stories, and memories of the families and, in some cases, the generations of families that once lived there.

Some of these places have since been converted into successful business establishments, allowing their owners to return the buildings to their original splendor and allowing the public an opportunity to drop in.

At the very terminal end of the peninsula, in the old whaling and fishing port of Provincetown, is Adams Pharmacy, a store with a connection to the nineteenth century. Located along storied Commercial Street, just a short jaunt from MacMillan Wharf and under the watchful stare of the Pilgrim Monument, Adams Pharmacy is the oldest continuously run business establishment in town. Built in the 1860s as a private home, the building became an apothecary as early as the 1870s. For a time it also was a doctor's office.

Along Skaket Beach Road in Orleans is the Captain Linnell House Restaurant, originally built in 1840 as a Cape Cod style house. A decade later the home was expanded by its owner, Captain Ebenezer Linnell, to resemble a house he once visited in Marseilles, France. This neo-classic French villa sported a copper roof with a cupola and widow's walk, Ionic pillars, Sandwich glass windows, and ceilings crafted from ship's knees.

Unfortunately, Captain Linnell - who set a sailing ship speed record with his 83 1/2-day voyage from London to Hong Kong in 1855 - would die at sea in a most gruesome way. While at the wheel of the clipper *Eagle Wing* in 1864, off the coast of South America, he was struck by the spanker sail, slamming him violently against the wheel. Besides cracking a number of ribs and breaking his collarbone, he was impaled on a spoke of the ship's wheel, puncturing his left lung.

Westward, along historic Route 6A in the village of Brewster is the Brewster Store. Serving as a Universalist Society church from 1852 to 1866, the building was sold to postmaster William Knowles who removed the steeple and opened a general store. The second

The Brewster Store, a fixture along Route 6A in that north side village, was once a church. (A. Sheedy photo)

floor, known as "The Hall," was used for village events while the main level housed the store and post office.

Knowles sold the store to Henry Crocker in 1925, who continued to operate it as a general store until 1947, at which time it passed to Donald Doane. In 1962, Doane turned the place into a museum, but later reopened it as a general store. After a couple of owner-ship changes the building saw structural renovations in 1990. Today, the first floor retains its general store atmosphere while the upstairs contains a collection of antiquities including the old Brewster Post Office and other items pointing to the town's past.

Situated in the heart of Yarmouthport village, along historic tree-lined Route 6A, is the Colonial House Inn. Built during the 1730s as a Federal style home by the Ryder family, it was a two-story structure with a hip roof. But a series of renovations, including the addition of a house that was sailed across the bay from Nantucket in the 1820s, began to alter its look. That Nantucket house was later divided in two during the 1860s and further repositioned within the existing dwelling. A third story was added and a Mansard roof replaced the original hip roof. Numerous other alterations both inside and out transformed the once Federal home into an elegant Victorian showplace.

The building remained a private home throughout the nine-teenth and into the twentieth centuries, owned by Eldridges, Thachers, Swifts, Brays, and Simpkins. After some years of neglect during the mid-twentieth century, the building was renovated in the 1980s and opened as an inn.

Hallet's Store, also on Route 6A in Yarmouthport, was built in 1889. It served the village as a drug store and soda fountain under the proprietorship of pharmacist T. T. Hallet, who was also post-master, justice of the peace, selectman, and collector of customs. The upstairs was used for town meetings. During the twentieth century, Hallet's became a small restaurant offering breakfast, lunch, dinner, and homemade ice cream.

To the south, near Bass River Bridge in the village of South Yarmouth, is the Bass River Mercantile. It is a living, breathing fragment of the nineteenth-century in the form of an old fashioned general store. Built circa 1810, perhaps by Quaker David Kelley, the building was most likely moved within the village to its present location around 1850. At that time South Yarmouth was largely a Quaker village. The old meetinghouse still stands, just up the road. The building that is today Bass River Mercantile has served as a family residence, a dry goods store, the South Yarmouth Post Office, and a pharmacy.

Along Route 6A in Barnstable Village, just up from the courthouse, rests the aptly named Barnstable House, built in 1716. It is an imposing colonial structure, especially at night when the reflection of the moon gives life to her upstairs windows. It's no wonder that the building is considered the most haunted building in town, claiming no less than 11 spirits!

Portions of the house were originally built in Scituate, Massachusetts and then moved by barge across the bay to its present location. James Paine, grandfather of Declaration of Independence signatory Robert Treat Paine, is credited with building the house. His family owned the dwelling for about six decades. Other owners included an Edmund Howes, who is believed to have hanged himself on the property, and a Dr. Samuel Savage, who was thought to have practiced black magic.

Perhaps the most popular of the building's ghost stories involves the Barnstable Fire Department. While battling a late-night fire that broke out in the top story of the structure during a snowstorm in the early 1970s, firemen noticed a blond haired woman wearing a Victorian-era dress in one of the upstairs windows. They made their way to her location, but she vanished, only to turn up outside levitating above the ground. After a few moments she disappeared completely.

Over the past century the place has served as an inn and a restaurant. In the 1930s it was known as Captain Grey's, serving lunch, dinner, and afternoon tea, and run by the De Witt Clintons. Today the Barnstable House is a professional building.

South again, in the village of Centerville, is a general store that recalls days of childhood when candy cost but a penny and comic books were only a dime. The 1856 Country Store of Centerville was actually built in the 1840s as a cranberry storage barn and later served as a shoe store. In 1856 it became a general mercantile, although it has also been used over the years as an antiques shop and an ice cream fountain. Nowadays it takes its place next to the old Congregational Church and cemetery of that south side village as a true Cape Cod original from its worn wooden floorboards to its potbelly stove.

Cape's Oldest Mill is Not on Cape Cod!

The use of windmills on Cape Cod is a natural product of prevailing winds and a practical application of technology. Whereas history documents only a handful of water-powered mills on the Cape, largely because there are too few streams with sufficient power to provide dependable water flow, references to numerous windmills are common.

There is evidence of windmill activity on Cape Cod as early as the end of the seventeenth century. Primarily utilized for grinding corn, these awkward structures (Thoreau referred to them as looking like large wounded birds!) served an important role in the economic and social life of Cape Cod villages.

For many years a windmill stood off Berry Avenue in West Yarmouth boasting a sign claiming that it was the oldest mill on

A postcard depiction of Yarmouth's Farris Mill, once the oldest windmill on Cape Cod. (J. Coogan collection)

Cape Cod. The actual origins of the mill are shrouded in some mystery, but most accounts have it in existence at the beginning of the 1700s, located in Yarmouthport near Cummaquid. There is even some conjecture that the mill originated in either Sandwich or West Barnstable in the mid-seventeenth century. A series of moves eventually took the mill to Bass River village at about the time of the American Revolution. In 1782, the mill was moved again to what is now called Mill Lane behind the South Yarmouth Methodist Church by Samuel Farris and Samuel Kelley and there it stayed for over a century.

Because the mill was operated for several generations by the Farris family, it came to be known as the Farris Mill. In 1894 it was purchased by a Mr. F. A. Abel who moved it to the West Yarmouth location off Berry Avenue. For the next quarter of a century the mill was featured in post cards as the oldest mill on Cape Cod.

In 1927, the Farris Mill was purchased from the Abel estate by Dr. Edward F. Gleason and was fully restored as years of neglect had caused the structure to fall into disrepair. The restored mill became an important tourist attraction for summer visitors to the West Yarmouth area. One of those attracted to the mill was Henry Ford. The well-known car manufacturer was at that time assembling his display of Americana at Dearborn Village in Michigan. A group of New England Ford dealers arranged to purchase the mill from Dr. Gleason as a gift for their corporate leader and in the fall of 1935 the structure was taken apart and, despite vigorous local protest, was trucked off to Michigan. By 1936 the mill was set on its new 10-foot stone foundation and ready for viewing.

And that is the curious story of why the oldest mill on Cape Cod is now located a few miles outside of Detroit!

The Barnstable Customs House

Built in 1856, the red brick building on Cobb Hill in Barnstable Village is known as the Trayser Museum. But it began life as a United States Customs House for the 7th U.S. Customs District, pointing to the busy harbor traffic of the nineteenth century.

Congressional approval for the construction of the customs

house was obtained through the efforts of Major Sylvanus B. Phinney, customs collector and *Barnstable Patriot* newspaper founder. The building also served as a post office. In fact, the hill upon which it sat was sometimes referred to as Post Office Hill.

Just a short jaunt from the harbor, the customs house served the port of Barnstable for nearly 60 years, registering and clearing vessels and collecting taxes until 1913. Owned at that time by the Federal Government, it remained a post office for the next 45 years, until 1958.

The town of Barnstable purchased the building for one dollar in 1960. Nowadays it is a museum, housing the collection of the Barnstable Historical Society. The main focus of the Society's collection is in preserving the town's proud maritime history, as evidenced by the telescopes, sextants, sail's loft equipment, and ship's logs on display.

The building is named for local historian Donald Trayser. Also on the grounds reside a fish shanty, a carriage house, and the old jail built around 1690, believed to be the oldest existing wooden jail building in the United States.

The old customs house in Barnstable village, now a museum. (A. Sheedy photo)

Once New England's Smallest Library?

There is some question as to whether the South Dennis Library was built where it currently stands or whether it was moved from some other location, perhaps from as far away as Wellfleet. Either way, the placard out front reads "circa 1856" - the estimated year of its construction.

First owned by a man named John Rose, regarded as Dennis' first Portuguese resident, the house eventually became home to two sisters, Elizabeth and Emily Smalle (an appropriate name given the miniature size of the dwelling). At the time its dimensions measured only 15 feet by 20 feet.

In 1918, it was sold to Captain Jonathan Matthews who later presented it to the town to be used as a library. For some time it was considered the smallest library in all of New England until a 16-foot by 26-foot addition was built in the mid-1960s. There was a library in Maine that might have been smaller.

A gingerbread woodwork design follows the gable end of the building to its peak. This decorative Gothic fretwork is repeated

South Dennis Library with its gingerbread fretwork. (A. Sheedy photo)

over the front door where an arched entrance leads inside. The front face features a pair of pointed tracery windows with pointed shutters to match. A small porch leading to the front door offers a pair of quatrefoils on the north and south walls.

Inside, clerestory latticework-style windows on each gable end of the room illuminate the bookshelves. Located near the librarian's desk is a door behind which is a steep set of stairs to two rooms seemingly hidden away for a century or more. In the front facing room are old books dating back into the 1800s ... delicate pages yellowed by age, each book blessed by the musty scent of history. In the other room is a closet with walls that have been papered with newsprint dating back to 1906. The Smalle sisters, it is believed, used this room as their lavatory ... and the newsprint provided them with plenty of bathroom reading material!

New Jerusalem

Recent renovations have helped save one of Yarmouth's, and one of the Cape's, most unique church buildings.

Along Route 6A in Yarmouthport, opposite the common, rests the Church of the New Jerusalem, also know as the New Church or the Swedenborgian Church. Stemming from the visions of Swedish scientist, philosopher, and theologian Emmanuel Swedenborg, who lived from 1688 to 1772, it draws its name from a passage in the Book of Revelations (Chapter 21, Verse 2: "And I John saw the holy city, the new Jerusalem, coming down out of heaven from God, prepared as a bride adorned for her husband"). Swedenborg received his revelations at the age of 55 and from those visions he reinterpreted various books of the Bible, verse by verse.

In 1784, the Swedenborgian church had its beginnings in England, spreading across the Atlantic to Baltimore in 1792. The church was incorporated in 1821 and arrived in Yarmouthport during the mid-1820s although it was not organized in town until the 1840s with nine founding members. One of the first in the town to join the New Church was Henry Thacher, a direct descendant of first comer Anthony Thacher. For a time church services were held in private homes, notably the home of Andrew Hallet. Beginning

The Swedenborgian Church, or Church of the New Jerusalem, from a turn of the century postcard. (J. Coogan collection)

in 1858, meetings took place on the second story of a Main Street store built by Swedenborgian James Knowles. That building now houses Parnassus Book Service.

The current church building, a unique structure that was designed by an Italian architect, was erected in 1870 with an official dedication on December 29. Reverend William H. Mayhew conducted the service, though records show that he was not installed as the church's pastor until November 1874. During the latter half of the nineteenth century the New Church became popular in town and its membership included a number of influential villagers.

Aaron's Folly

Resting on Town Cove in Orleans, right next to the historic Jonathan Young Windmill, is one of the most interesting buildings in the area. Known today as the Orleans Inn, it was at one time jokingly referred to as "Aaron's Folly."

The building began life as a private residence, built by Captain Aaron Snow. The Snow family has had an identity on Cape Cod right back to the time of the Pilgrims. In fact, Aaron Snow was a direct descendant of Constance Hopkins, who came over on the *Mayflower* in 1620. With permission granted by Governor William Bradford himself, Constance and her husband Nicholas Snow along with six other families later relocated from Plimoth to the lower Cape region of Nauset. From these humble beginnings some 350 years ago came the Snows of Orleans.

Aaron Snow was born in 1825. He married a Mary Tutty and the couple had seven children. Approaching age 50, Aaron got the notion to build a home on the cove unlike any other in town. He had lumber shipped down from Maine to his dock and set off to work. Meanwhile, the townsfolk watched and wondered what Captain Snow was building. Was it a house? Was it a commercial building? Was it a hotel? Townsfolk dubbed the building "Aaron's Folly" and watched and waited some more as Captain Snow took his time piecing the place together.

Finally, in 1875, the project was completed. It was, in fact, a private residence consisting of some 14 rooms. The property also included a number of sheds and a wharf built of lumber scavenged from a local shipwreck. At the wharf he docked his schooner *Nettie M. Rogers* upon which he carried cargoes in the manner of coal, lumber, whale oil, and grain. On the property he also ran a general store.

The building was used as the Snow's private residence until 1892, during which year both Captain Snow and his wife Mary died just months apart. At that time, sons Aaron, William, and George took possession of the building and later sold it for $1,000 to an Abner Rogers at auction in 1895. It later passed to a Charles Amadon around the turn of the century, to an Edwin Ellis around 1912, and to a Mary Linnell in the 1920s who ran the place as a boarding house. It was still being used as a boarding house in the 1940s. During the war years the northeast and southwest wings were added to the main building. In later years the place became a summer resort and a restaurant.

Tales of mobsters of the past and ghostly apparitions of the present have been attached to the Orleans Inn. Some say that the building was used as a "cooling off" place for Boston area mobsters some 40 or 50 years ago. These mobsters would fly down to the Cape and hide out at the inn while things calmed down up in the city. As for the hauntings, stories of candles re-lighting by themselves, doors slamming and unlocking under their own power, the sound of footsteps, cold spots and even the occasional sighting of an apparition abound. One ghost is thought to be that of a woman of questionable reputation who may have died at the inn perhaps a half century ago. Though her identity is unknown, she is affectionately called "Hannah" by the staff.

As the decades have proven, one man's folly is another man's castle. The Orleans Inn has survived various incarnations over the years to arrive today, in the beginning years of the twenty-first century, as a striking Orleans landmark now run as an inn, a restaurant, and a tavern. Its Victorian visage and towering cupola peer out over the cove, keeping a watchful eye on the goings on about town.

Aaron's Folly, now better known as the Orleans Inn. (J. Sheedy photo)

Cape Cod Skyscraper

Cape Cod is not known for tall buildings. One of the most remarkable structures ever seen on the Cape was the Harwich Exchange Building, which was dedicated on March 31, 1885 in Harwich Center. The building was located on the corner of Route 124 and Main Street and was 58 feet wide, 100 feet long, and, including its foundation of 100,000 Barnstable bricks, stood 104 feet high from the top of the cupola to the ground. That's about 10 stories! Outside of the Provincetown Monument, it was the tallest building ever constructed on Cape Cod.

"The Exchange," as it was known by local residents, was a mercantile center for the mid-Cape region. It stood on the site of another large building that had served the same purpose, which had burned in 1876. There were four working floors in the building. The first level housed two large retail establishments. On the second floor there was a large meeting hall and auditorium that, with its balcony, could seat 1,000 people. Perhaps even more incredible, the third floor was the site of an octagon shaped rock-maple floored roller skating rink that could handle as many as 200 skaters.

A fourth floor was used as storage area with full headroom and from which access could be made to the glass-enclosed cupola. Mariners passing down Nantucket Sound used this observation tower as a navigation point for many years. Below, the massive basement was said to be able to store 5,000 barrels of cranberries.

The building featured 25 stained glass windows and utilized gas generated lighting. Homegrown coffee magnate Caleb Chase of West Harwich paid off the mortgage on the building in 1903 and presented the Exchange Building as a gift to the town.

In 1964, facing great costs of maintenance and upkeep on this huge property, Harwich voters reluctantly decided to demolish it. On November 17 of that year demolition began and by January of 1965 the site of the Exchange Building, which served the town for almost 80 years, became a vacant lot.

Chapter
11

Turn of the Century

If a photographer could have taken pictures around Cape Cod in 1650, 1750, and 1850, the images would not have shown a great deal of difference. In the pre-industrial period, Cape Cod remained for two centuries a rural area, relying on the sea for sustenance and transportation. The homogeneous nature of the culture was reinforced by the region's relative isolation from the rest of Massachusetts.

The post Civil War period, although affected by cycles of economic decline and out migration, saw dramatic changes that were precursors to what the twentieth century would bring. The railroad opened the Cape to newcomers and by the end of the nineteenth century a solid base of summer tourism filled the guesthouses and pockets of Cape Codders. The novels of Joseph C. Lincoln focused attention on the characters and the culture of Cape Cod. Perhaps longing for the roots they had left behind in their move inland to the growing urban centers of the Midwest, millions of Americans looked at Lincoln's images of small town life along the seacoast with nostalgia and interest. Thousands came to Cape

Cod to see for themselves what it was about.

As technology changed and people "from away" began to discover Cape Cod, it was inevitable that the narrow land would, itself, morph into something quite different than what it had been in earlier days. Still, the charm and atmosphere of the Cape, with its quaint little villages and interesting characters brought people who might have wanted, as Thoreau said, to get just a bit "salted." The new century brought visitors who enjoyed having a bit of that salt rub off on them and they returned in ever increasing numbers.

From railroads, traffic rotaries, up to date phone systems, and even pioneer aviators, Cape Cod had arrived in the modern age.

Along the Cape Cod Railroad

The railroad that eventually made its way to Cape Cod had its beginnings back in 1844 when the Old Colony Railroad was initially chartered to connect Boston to Plymouth. Trains ran between Boston and Providence since 1835, and to New Bedford since 1840. The line to Plymouth was opened in November 1845. Within three years, the railroad was extended from Middleboro to Sandwich, thus bringing the steam engine to Cape Cod.

A day of festivities met the opening of the Sandwich station on May 26, 1848. The gigantic train roundhouse at the station became the second tallest building in town. Only the spire of the Congregational Church was taller. Regular passenger and freight service commenced three days later, with freight charges running about $1.50 per ton. Stagecoaches, which at one time transported travelers to the Cape, now met the trains at the station to whisk passengers off to their local destinations. The mail, also at one time arriving on Cape via stagecoach, was now delivered by rail as well. The packet and coaster businesses also began to suffer in the face of this new competition as the railroad slowly made its way across the peninsula.

The Cape Cod Branch Railroad, later known as the Cape Cod Central Railroad, extended its reach to Barnstable by May 1854, and further to Yarmouth and south to Hyannis by later that same year. Hyannis met the arrival of the railroad with a celebration including a band concert and a cannon salute. Eight trains per day arrived at Hyannis. Steamers of the Fall River Line, operated by the Old Colony, made the run from Hyannis to the islands of Nantucket and Martha's Vineyard. In this way, passengers could step onto a train at Boston, and then at Hyannis right onto an awaiting ferry for the final leg of the journey to their island destination.

Meanwhile to the north, a station was erected at the corner of Cross and Railroad streets in Yarmouthport to unload a growing crop of tourists, and to load Cape Cod products for transport to off-Cape vendors. The Yarmouthport station was serviced by five trains a day from Boston. Further eastward spread the rails, reaching Orleans in 1865, Wellfleet in 1870, and finally terminating at Provincetown in 1873. The previous year a track was laid south from Sandwich to Woods Hole, making that port the terminus for connections to the islands, redirecting the ferry business from the port of Hyannis.

As early as 1863, the residents of Chatham were talking about a railway to their town. Yet, the tracks that arrived at Orleans from Harwich in 1865 bypassed the elbow of the Cape. Well into the 1880s a stagecoach was still servicing Chatham with a daily run from Harwich, otherwise the town was virtually cut off from the

Provincetown station around the turn of the twentieth century. (J. Coogan collection)

rest of the Cape towns, all of which had train service except for
Mashpee.

Finally, in 1887, ties cut from Maine trees were shipped to the
Cape for the purposes of building a spur to the seemingly forgotten township. The rail was opened in November of that year, with
Chatham boasting a Victorian depot, an engine house, a turntable,
a car house, and a well with a windmill to pump water for the
steam engines. Fare for the 12-minute run from Harwich cost 35
cents. On the opening day of operation, a load of cranberries was
the railway's first freight shipment out of Chatham.

Meanwhile, the wealthy of Falmouth had their own train, called
the Flying Dude. From 1884 to 1914, this train made the run from
Boston to Woods Hole. For 14 of those years her conductor was
Augustus Messer, who was also conductor of the first train to
reach Woods Hole in 1872. Commuters, largely consisting of
businessmen who worked in Boston during the week, shelled out
$100 for a summer's worth of passages to the Cape in order to be
with their families for the weekend.

In 1893, the New York, New Haven and Hartford Railroad
signed a 99-year lease with the Old Colony Railroad for use of the
464 miles of track and equipment. Unfortunately, the full 99 years
would not be needed as a new mode of transportation was threat-
ening the railroad just as the railroad had threatened numerous
horse-drawn and seagoing modes of transportation over a half
century before. After the turn of the twentieth century the automobile arrived on Cape Cod, and with it came a whole new feeling of
independence. No longer did tourists need to consider train
schedules and connecting carriages, as the automobile provided
the driver with complete control of his journey from departure to
arrival, and any stops along the way.

Though trains would continue to carry the bulk of freight to the
Cape into the 1950s, passenger service was curtailed beginning in
1930. During that year, service to Chatham was cut to two trips per
day, and then later the Chatham station was closed altogether as
service between that town and Harwich was ended after some 40
years of operation. It took just one month to tear up the tracks that
had taken two decades of lobbying to acquire. Passenger rail

service to South Yarmouth, South Dennis and consequently to all points east was ceased in 1938. The Yarmouthport station remained open, and was essentially the end of the line save for the rail south to Hyannis. From the late-1940s to the mid-1950s a sparkling red train named the "Cranberry" made the run to Boston.

By 1958, the announcement was made to discontinue Cape passenger rail service due to multi-million dollar losses. Automobiles were the new wave, and the 1956 Federal Aid Highway Act, providing tax dollars for highway improvement, sounded the death knell. A million-dollar subsidy paid by the 38 communities serviced by the railroad kept it up and running for another year, although it would not be enough to turn the tide. On June 30, 1959 the last year-round passenger trains left Cape Cod. Summer service from June to Labor Day continued to run from 1960 to 1964, with the "Cape Codder" making daily six-hour trips between New York and Hyannis; the "Neptune" making the weekend run. Yet, even this limited service was discontinued due to the railroad's continued unsteady financial situation.

Today the rails from Hyannis to Yarmouth and west to the Canal are still in use, during the summer months for excursions and all year long to transport trash off-Cape. Eastward, from South Dennis, the Cape Cod bike trail traces the original path of the railroad, two-wheelers now silently gliding where locomotives once chugged.

First in Flight?

In the years just prior to the twentieth century there was a great interest in the idea that man could fly. The eventual success of the Wright brothers in fulfilling that dream may well be attributed to the skill and craftsmanship of a simple Chatham carpenter.

James A. Crowell was a self-styled "Jack of all trades" with a home near the Mill Pond in Chatham. One of his summer neighbors was Samuel Cabot of Boston. Cabot had developed an interest in human flight while traveling in Europe. There he saw German glider craft soaring along the edges of the Alps. Cabot purchased the plans for these gliders and brought them back to the United

States. He engaged Mr. Crowell to help him build the airframes for the flying craft in his barn.

Crowell described the gliders he built as being "birdlike" in design. The frames were made out of hollow hard pine rods and covered with Japanese silk. Each machine was about 15 feet long and five feet wide. The seat for the pilot was hung below the frame and the aviator, or "scaler" as Crowell described it, had to run down the side of a hill and jump into the seat as the craft took to the sky. It took great balance and stamina to get into the air for these short glides that lasted a matter of seconds. "If we went 50 feet we thought it was a real good flight," Crowell recalled years later.

Mr. Cabot was usually the pilot of the gliders, but occasionally Crowell took the controls himself. He would launch from Morris Island or the Mill Pond hills depending on the wind direction. The preferable landing area was the water because it was softer than the hard sandy hills that surrounded the launching sites. In efforts to chart the wind currents of the launching area, Cabot had Crowell construct many kites to fly so that wind direction could be recorded.

The two men worked together for almost 30 years in pursuit of what was probably more of a hobby than anything else. "We got a machine that looked a lot like the aeroplanes do today, before we got through," said Crowell years after Cabot's death and long after they had given up the sport. "A feller in Washington wanted my model, the last one I had, so I let him take it. Mr. Cabot sold the patents to a couple of brothers, lived out west somewhere. One of them died – I forget their name."

Could the two brothers have been Orville and Wilbur? It's hard to be sure.

There is no monument in Chatham to James A. Crowell as a pioneer aviator, but his skill and courage was certainly a contributing factor to the success of later and more famous knights of the air.

Speed Trap!

It was a nice clear afternoon on July 5, 1905 when Mr. J. L.

Bachelder, Jr. was driving his car through Sandwich on his way to his summer home in Osterville. He had his family with him and as he motored down the county road his anticipation of the wonderful vacation days ahead of him perhaps caused him to stray above the speed limit.

Suddenly, out of the bushes along the roadway jumped Sandwich Police Officer Andrew Higgins who flagged down the surprised "autoist" and handed him a ticket for speeding. It seems that Bachelder's car had exceeded the speed limit of 15 miles per hour in the outskirts of the town. The first Cape Cod speed trap had captured a victim!

Anyone who today regularly drives the Mid-Cape Highway knows where the police have set up traps to catch motorists who drive too fast. Crackdowns on car speeding don't cause much of a ripple among the driving public nowadays. But in 1905 the whole concept of automobiles running amuck on Cape Cod was almost unheard of. There were only a few thousand cars operating in the entire state in that dawn of the auto age. In Sandwich, however, the town selectmen, in their wisdom, saw a chance to catch the unwary speeding travelers and at the same time enrich the town treasury. Thus was hatched the scheme that put Officer Higgins in

Early twentieth century postcard showing the "state highway, Cape Cod, Mass." (J. Coogan collection)

the bushes by the side of the road.

A few weeks after the incident, Mr. Bachelder, accompanied by his lawyer, appeared in Barnstable District Court before Judge Swift. Bachelder pleaded not guilty and based his defense on the fact that he had been cited for speeding in an area that had always allowed speeds up to 20 miles per hour. His lawyer asked that the case be dismissed because his client could not possibly have known of any change in the law. Sandwich officials admitted that they had officially changed the speed limit on June 15 so that the 15-mile-per-hour limit applied to roads that extended beyond the outskirts of the village. The vote was made at the spring town meeting, but signs had never been put up to alert motorists. Judge Swift discharged the defendant stating that, under the circumstances, Mr. Bachelder could not be held.

There was quite a bit of reaction over the dismissal of this speeding case. People outside of Sandwich had little sympathy for the town, which claimed that they lost money enforcing the speed laws. A commentator from Fall River noted, "In their efforts to regulate the speed at which automobilists can drive their machines through cities and towns, there is a danger that the authorities may proceed to a degree quite as much beyond reason as the disposition displayed by some of the scorchers."

Judge Nathan Washborn of Middleboro chided Sandwich officials saying, "I want to find out what this spasmodic attempt in Sandwich over automobiles means. If it is to replenish the town treasury, I do not think they have succeeded."

Still, there was an acknowledgement that excessive speed needed to be controlled and that 20 miles an hour was certainly fast enough for anyone. The same Fall River critic admitted, "The public highways are no places for record-breaking trials. There is a spirit of carelessness bordering on cruelty in dashing past a fractious horse, indifferent of the consequences to the driver, or in rushing pell-mell through the crowded streets of a city or town."

Thus it was that Sandwich's attempt at controlling the "scorchers" passing through the town failed in the summer of 1905. As a result of Mr. Bachelder's acquittal, the town had to forfeit over $300 in anticipated fines.

The Great Hyannis Fire of 1904

A terrible fire would visit Hyannis on the evening of December 3, 1904 and would leave 600 feet along Main Street's north side in ashes. Damages amounted to somewhere in the neighborhood of $150,000, of which only about half was insured.

Just around midnight the fire was discovered by L. P. Wilson who, with his wife, two children and mother, lived above his store, the Hyannis Public Market. The cause was never determined and there was great debate over whose building, whether Wilson's market or Walter Baker's department store, was the origin of the terrible destruction to follow.

Church bells rang out into the night to alert the fire department. At the nearby train depot locomotive whistles were blown. According to the December 5th issue of *The Barnstable Patriot*, even Mr. M. M. Garmon got into the act, riding through the streets atop a horse belonging to a Mr. Soule, calling out to the residents of Hyannis like some early-twentieth century Paul Revere.

The Hyannis Fire Department responded immediately with two double-cylinder chemical engines, two hose carriages and "a well-equipped hook and ladder" according to the *Patriot*. Unfortunately, the fire had a significant head start and was heavily involved when the fire brigade arrived. Baker's store was the first to go, followed by each successive building to the west. Many of the structures were built only a few feet apart, allowing the fire to tear its way along Main Street without hesitation. Calls for assistance were sent out as far away as Provincetown and Brockton.

Consumed by the flames, besides Wilson's Hyannis Public Market and Baker's department store, were Richardson Brothers Photography, William P. Bearse & Company Meats and Provision, and P.F. Campbell & Company Tailors. Along with the Megathlin Building went Chas. W. Megathlin Drug and Medicine, the Singer Sewing Machine Company on the ground floor, and the New England Telephone Exchange on the second story.

Postmaster Goss was able to save all the first class mail and the safe before the post office fell to the flames. Other casualties included F.H. Bassett's grocery store, Julia Stevens' dressmaking shop, James E. Baxter's shoe store, Thomas W. Nickerson's marble and granite business, and Augustus B. Nye's paint shop. Nye lost his earlier paint shop in an 1892 fire. This latest inferno was Nye's third fire in the span of 12 years!

The largest building to fall to the flames was the Eagleston Building in which A.P. & E.L. Eagleston's dry goods, furniture, and carpet store was located. Sparks and flames fell all about the street, causing some $3,000 damage to nearby buildings, including a number of structures on the south side of Main Street, though those buildings were spared. Not spared, sadly, was the building resting just west of the Eagleston Building. That edifice, the last to surrender to the flames of the Hyannis Fire of 1904, was the First Universalist Church.

For a moment it looked as if the church might escape destruction, as there was quite a distance between the Eagleston Building and the church building. But it was not to be. The flames from the Eagleston Building leapt 30 to 40 feet between the two structures to ignite the church. The clock on the spire stopped at five minutes before three o'clock, the moment when the clock's innards incinerated and the giant steeple came crashing down to Main Street below.

The fire resulted in one fatality. Captain William Penn Lewis suffered a stroke while attempting to save his house from the flames.

In true Yankee spirit, Postmaster Goss was ready for business at 5 o'clock that morning. He had relocated the Post Office to the parlor of Mrs. E.C. Benson's house at the corner of Main and Pleasant streets. Many others burned out of their establishments were open for business at different locations during the course of the weeks to follow. Over the ensuing months, the northeast end of Main Street was rebuilt.

Labor Day Hotel Fires of Hyannisport

At the turn of the century, Hyannisport was in its heyday as a resort for well-to-do summer visitors. Legendary summerhouses and cottages opened their doors for another season of beach parties, croquet matches, and evening dances. Also opening their doors to the summer season were Hyannisport's two popular hotels, the Hallett House at the corner of Wachusett Avenue and Longwood and the Port View Hotel on nearby Irving Avenue.

Hallett House, built in 1873 by retired sea captain Gideon Hallett, was the "Port's" first hotel. Three stories high, it contained two bowling alleys, a billiard and poolroom, and accommodations for 100 guests. It was considered *the* place to stay at Hyannisport. Local newspapers would announce who had arrived off the train that week to stay at the Hallett House ... it was high society Cape Cod style.

An advertisement in the *1880 Atlas of Barnstable County* lists Hallett as the proprietor of the "summer house." Mrs. Emily Whelden replaced Hallett in 1888 and was proprietress in 1905 when the Hallett House enjoyed its most successful summer in terms of receipts. That wonderful 1905 summer season was nearly over when disaster struck.

On September 5, Labor Day, a fire was discovered in the men's washroom at 7:15 p.m. At the time the hotel was full with visitors, having just finished their dinners in the Hallett House dining room and now upstairs preparing for an 8 o'clock dance. The fire spread quickly, and earlier thoughts of saving valuables and luggage were dashed in favor of saving lives.

Local church bells were rung to alert the Hyannis Fire Brigade, but their efforts were in vain. Though all lives were spared, the hotel was completely destroyed. A partial insurance policy did not provide enough funds to rebuild. Hyannisport had lost its exclusive hotel.

Remarkably, a similar event occurred at the Port View Hotel on Labor Day evening in 1909. Again, the summer season had come to a close and visitors were no doubt sitting on the Port View porch overlooking the waves of Hyannis Harbor and Nantucket Sound beyond, reminiscing about the fire that had claimed the Hallett House just four Labor Days earlier. The Port View, though three stories and featuring a waterfront location, was not considered as elegant as Hallett House, but by attrition it had become Hyannisport's hotel of choice.

Built in the 1880s, the Port View, at the easternmost end of Irving Avenue, became a landmark on the Hyannisport waterfront. The hotel was situated right at the beginning of the boardwalk and can be seen in many of the old "Port" pictures. Miss Martha Keough operated Port View on that Labor Day evening in 1909 when a fire broke out in the dining room around 9 o'clock. As with the Hallett House blaze four years earlier, all souls escaped the inferno though the building was an utter loss. Damages totaled $10,000 and insufficient insurance did not allow the owners to rebuild.

Cape Cod Canal – A Pilgrim's Dream

Cape Cod is a peninsula of unparalleled beauty. Actually, to be more accurate, Cape Cod was once a peninsula, as for the past century it has been an island, cut off from the mainland of Massachusetts by an eight and a half-mile long, 500-foot wide waterway known as the Cape Cod Canal.

To understand the story of the canal and how it came into being one must look both to its history and its geography. The Indians appreciated the importance of what was known as the Manomet Valley and the waterways that swept through it. From Cape Cod Bay they would paddle south along Scusset Creek for about two miles and then travel by foot two to three miles to reach the Manomet River, where they would canoe another two or three miles to Buzzards Bay. In this way, they could traverse the Cape with a minimal hike over land using the two waterways to their advantage.

In 1623, Pilgrim Captain Myles Standish took advantage of this shortcut as well. Within four years the Pilgrims built a trading post, named Aptucxet, along the banks of the Manomet River to facilitate trade with the Dutch at New Amsterdam as well as with the Narragansett Indians. The Pilgrims bartered for furs, which were then sent to England to pay off their debt with the Merchant Adventurers of London, financiers of the *Mayflower* expedition. Some 14,000 pounds of furs were sent in the year 1634 alone.

It was during these early years that Pilgrim William Bradford first considered the idea of a canal to "avoyd the compasing of Cap-Codd, and those deangerous shoulds, and so make any vioage to ye southward in much shorter time, and with farr less danger." Standish determined the canal should be eight feet wide and four feet deep to accommodate their boats. Yet, no canal was dug and the notion remained only that, a notion for centuries to come. It was, though, a notion that would resurface many times over the next three centuries until shovel finally met earth.

In 1698, a committee was formed to consider the proposal of digging a canal, although nothing came of it. With British troops blockading the northeast ports of Boston and New York, General Washington ordered a survey of the area in 1776 and sent one of his chief engineers, Thomas Machin, to make his assessment of a possible canal. Machin recommended a seven and a half-mile long, 14-foot deep waterway with a lock at each end, to cost £32,148, one shilling and eight pence. Unfortunately, Washington recalled Machin, as his engineering skills were needed elsewhere and the canal remained unearthed.

By 1812, the country was once again at war with the British, whose warships were making it difficult for American mariners attempting to move cargoes along the coast. After the war, a September 1815 hurricane and the accompanying storm surge nearly joined the waters of Scusset Creek and Manomet River, briefly creating by nature what mankind had considered for nearly two centuries yet never attempted.

Further discussion continued from 1818 through 1830 as the government opened up the building of a canal to private investors, but talk and more talk was all that resulted. The town of Sandwich, the canal's major proponent, believed that along with an inland waterway would come prosperity. Yet, all thought of a canal was shelved during the middle part of the nineteenth century as Sandwich Glassworks, founded in 1825, made the former sleepy village of farmers one of the richest towns on Cape. All appeared well in the town of Sandwich, even without a canal.

As the railroad arrived on Cape Cod the need for a ship canal diminished further. Meanwhile, clipper ships took most seagoing business far away from Cape Cod shores in favor of trade with foreign ports. And the steam engine appeared to provide mariners with the machinery necessary to successfully and safely navigate the local waters.

Yet, by 1870 interest in a waterway resurfaced. Interestingly, the *1880 Atlas of Barnstable County* shows a "Proposed Ship Canal" snaking its way across the map of Sandwich, running from Monument (Manomet) River eastward to Scusset Harbor. During that period, the Cape Cod Ship Canal Company was formed and in the 1880s hundreds of Italian immigrants arrived from New York City to move earth for less than $1 per day in pay. Over time the company went bankrupt, and after a brief period of turmoil termed the "Neapolitan Revolt," the Italians returned to New York. Another attempt in the early 1890s excavated a ditch over one mile in length, 100 feet in width and some 15 feet in depth. Again, work halted when money ran out.

The nineteenth century had all but escaped without a workable canal proposal when the Boston, Cape Cod and New York Canal Company was formed. Heading up this latest venture was De Witt Clinton Flanagan, who recruited August Belmont as financier. Belmont had been instrumental in the building of the New York subway system, and the canal project seemed to be a perfect match. Besides, Belmont, whose maternal grandfather was Commodore Matthew Perry, had ties to the Perrys of Bourne. He subsequently bought out Flanagan and set off to the work of designing what would become one of the world's greatest canals.

Since the time of Washington and throughout the nineteenth century the talk had always been of a canal with locks, because the tides at Cape Cod Bay are five feet higher than those at Buzzards Bay. Adding to the headaches was the fact that Buzzards Bay experienced high tide three hours earlier than Cape Cod Bay. Consequently, the current of a canal connecting these two bodies of water would be quite swift. Regardless, Belmont wanted to build a sea level canal without locks. His engineers determined that such a waterway should be 25 feet deep with a bottom width of 100 feet and a surface width of 200 feet to minimize the speed of the current.

Work began in 1909 and continued for five years. The project cost Belmont about $13 million. In 1911, the Bourne Bridge was opened to traffic, followed in 1913 by the Sagamore Bridge and the railroad bridge, all three drawbridges. In April 1914, dikes were opened allowing waters from the north and south to meet. By July of that year the Cape Cod Canal was operating at a depth of 15 feet. After two more years of dredging, the canal finally reached the 25-foot depth requirement. For seafarers willing to pay the 10-cent per ton toll they could avoid the "back shore run" around the Cape and thereby reduce their voyage by some 70 miles.

Belmont's control over his waterway was short lived. With America's involvement in World War I and increased German submarine activity along the northeast coast, including a U-boat attack that sank four barges off Orleans, the U.S. Railroad Administration stepped in to operate the canal. When the war ended the government attempted to hand control back over to Belmont, but he wanted no part of it. Negotiations went on for years, and a payment of $11.5 million to his estate, four years after Belmont's death in 1924, did not equal the estimated $16 million Belmont had sunk into the initial building of the canal and its subsequent dredging.

Major improvements were made from 1932 to 1940. The depth was increased to 34 feet and the bottom was widened to 480 feet making it the world's widest sea level canal. The total length was increased to 17.4 miles including the approaches through Buzzards Bay and Cape Cod Bay. The present bridges were all constructed during this period, two continuous truss highway bridges over 600

Activity along the Cape Cod Canal – a pleasure boat in the foreground and a tug pushing a barge toward the Sagamore Bridge. (A. Sheedy photo)

feet in length and a vertical lift railroad bridge 544 feet in length, the latter being the longest bridge of its type in the world. All three bridges offered 135 feet of vertical clearance.

Today, the Cape Cod Canal is operated by the U.S. Army Corps of Engineers who use a sophisticated array of radio, radar, and closed circuit television systems to monitor traffic. It is truly a manmade masterpiece. Its graceful, curving flow traces the path that the Pilgrims envisioned nearly 400 years ago when Standish considered a four-foot deep waterway. Though the scale is grander, the dream that finally brought it to fruition was very much the same.

The First Traffic Rotary

Every time your heart begins to beat fearfully as you grip your steering wheel and try to gain a smooth entrance to one of Cape Cod's traffic rotaries, you can thank a South Yarmouth man for giving us the idea of a managed circular traffic flow.

Charles Henry Davis, who lived in what was at one time called "The House of Seven Chimneys" along Bass River, was an early advocate for a national highway system. In 1912, he formed the National Highway Association to lobby the government for better roads in the early age of automobile travel. He was a colorful figure on Cape Cod. As a yachtsman he was master of travel on water. But it was land travel that he most wanted to improve.

He drove a car that displayed all of the state license plates from around the nation and in this period he established what many believe is one of the first traffic rotaries in the United States near his home at the intersection of River and Pleasant streets.

The site of this still-functioning rotary is where an early horse watering trough once stood. In a time when cars still went slow enough to read street signs, lanterns were hung from the main post in the center of the circular brick rotary. Signs told drivers where they were headed and it was seen as a marvel of innovative traffic management.

Today, in the world of cutthroat driving, when few people understand the meaning of the word "yield," traffic rotaries are the source of fear and loathing among drivers. Many would characterize them as "vicious circles" that can lead to a near-death experience. Traffic surveys indicate that most motorists would get rid of them in a minute.

Davis' dream of a national highway system did eventually come true and many rotaries still remain on Cape Cod. Interestingly, there is a rotary at the entrance to West Dennis Beach, a piece of valuable land that was donated by Mr. Davis for recreation use by local inhabitants. In 1999, a modified rotary called a "roundabout" was put in place at Route 149 and Race Lane in Barnstable. The jury is still out as to whether this will be an improvement in the traffic flow there.

Blame it on Hoover

You have to feel a bit sorry for President Herbert Hoover. After a brilliant record as head of European World War I famine relief under the U.S. Food Administration and a successful career in the U.S. Commerce Department, Hoover became President in time for the beginning of the economic collapse that ushered in the Great Depression.

He was blamed for just about everything that went wrong in those difficult years. Even on Cape Cod the thirty-first President came in for criticism. It seems that shortly after becoming President in 1928, Hoover signed into law a national standard for bricks. The West Barnstable Brick Company, which had hit a peak production of over 100,000 bricks a day in 1927, found itself with brick-making equipment that produced bricks smaller than the new national standard. The company, which had been in operation since 1878, was forced to invest money in new equipment to make the two-inch by four-inch by eight-inch bricks that were required by Hoover's new law. The Barnstable bricks, it seems, were one-eighth of an inch too short!

In order to cover its costs, the company raised prices on its bricks just as the economy began its downward slide. Eventually it lost its share of the market and was forced into bankruptcy in 1933 when the First National Bank of Yarmouth called in a $30,000 loan, never to re-open. Since it was a significant employer of workers in the

West Barnstable and Sandwich area, the impact was especially felt in the upper Cape. "Hoover Bricks" became part of the local language of the Great Depression, along with the more widely used "Hoover Blankets" and "Hoovervilles."

Spring in Hyannis ... All Year Long

Before the 1950s, to make a telephone call on Cape Cod you cranked the old Western Electric machine and a real live local person asked, "Number please?" This person was efficient enough for small town communications in a time when most people made calls from the local post office and almost never used the phone at night.

In the mid-1950s, the Telephone Company began the process of switching to automated exchanges on Cape Cod. In a move designed to make the move more attractive to people who saw no need to give up a tried and true system, the people at Bell tried to create fancy sounding names for dialing areas. The intent seemed to be that the fancier the name, the more likely the people would feel comfortable with the new system. Hyannis was SPRING, Barnstable Village and much of the north side of the mid-Cape was FOREST (fairly appropriate for the time). South Yarmouth and West Dennis had the name EXETER and Osterville could be rung up as GARDEN.

To place a call to Falmouth you dialed KIMBALL and for Bourne it was PLAZA. It took a bit longer to automate the lower Cape, but the names were just as good. Brewster became TWIN OAKS, and Wellfleet was FIELDBROOK, (BOUND BROOK would have been a much better name!). The remaining towns came on line by the mid-1960s, but by that time the practice of inventing fancy names for dialing areas was pretty much out of fashion.

Today we are left to use our own imaginations in creating a fancy message for our answering machines, all the while hoping that when we pick up the phone we might get lucky and actually be able to talk to a real live telephone operator.

BIBLIOGRAPHY

Archer, Gleason L. Mayflower Heroes. New York, NY: The Century Company, 1931.

Archer, Gleason L. With Axe and Musket at Plymouth. New York, NY: The American Historical Society, Inc., 1936.

Barnard, Ruth L. A History of Orleans. Taunton, MA: William S. Sullwold Publishing, 1975.

Barnstable County. Three Centuries of a Cape Cod County: Barnstable, Massachusetts, 1685-1985. Barnstable, MA: Barnstable County, 1985.

Beston, Henry. The Outermost House. Garden City, NY: Doubleday, Doran & Co, Inc, 1929.

Bingham, Amelia. Mashpee: Land of the Wampanoags. Mashpee, MA: Mashpee Centennial Committee, 1970.

Bodensiek, Fred. Barnstable at 350. Barnstable, MA: Barnstable 350th Committee, 1989.

Bradford, William. Bradford's History "of Plymouth Plantation." Boston, MA: Wright & Potter Printing Co, 1898.

Bray, Mary Mathews. A Sea Trip in Clipper Ship Days.

Brigham, Albert Perry. Cape Cod and the Old Colony. New York, NY: Grosset & Dunlap, 1920.

Burrows, Fredrika A. Windmills on Cape Cod and the Islands. Taunton, MA: Wm. S. Sullwold Publishing, Inc., 1978.

Butterworth Company. Cape Cod & Islands Atlas. West Yarmouth, MA.

Cabral, Reginald W. Wooden Ships and Iron Men. Provincetown, MA: Trustees of the Provincetown Heritage Museum, 1994.

Carpenter, Delores Bird. Early Encounters. East Lansing, MI: Michigan State University Press, 1994.

Carpenter, Edmund J., The Pilgrims and Their Monument. New York, NY: D. Appleton and Co., 1911.

Cataldo, Louis. Pictorial Tales of Cape Cod. Hyannis, MA: Tales of Cape Cod, Inc, 1956.

Chatham, Dennis & Marion. Cape Coddities. Boston, MA & New York, NY: Houghton Mifflin Co, 1920.

Cheever, George B. The Journal of the Pilgrims at Plymouth in New England – 1620. New York, NY: John Wiley, 1848.

Clark, Admont G. Lighthouses of Cape Cod, Martha's Vineyard, Nantucket. East Orleans, MA: Parnassus Imprint, 1992.

Clark, Admont G. They Built Clipper Ships in Their Back Yard. Yarmouthport, MA: Parnassus Imprint, 1963.

Corbett, Scott. We Chose Cape Cod. New York, NY: Thomas Y. Crowell Co, 1953.

Crosby, Katharine. Blue-Water Men & Other Cape Codders. New York, NY: The Macmillan Company, 1946.

Crowell, Levi. History of Levi Crowell as Written by Himself Including the Diary of His Incarceration in a Confederate Prison. West Dennis, MA: William Smith Ryder, Jr., 1990.

Cullity, Rosanna and John Nye. A Sandwich Album. Sandwich, MA: Nye Family of America Society, 1987.

Dalton, J.W. The Lifesavers of Cape Cod. Chatham, MA: The Chatham Press, Inc., 1967.

Darling, Edward. Three Old Timers of Cape Cod. Hyannis, MA: Wake-Brook House, 1974.

Davis, William T. Plymouth Memories of an Octogenarian. Plymouth, MA: The Memorial Press, 1906.

Deyo, Simeon L. History of Barnstable County, Massachusetts 1620-1890. New York, NY: H.W. Blake & Co, 1890.

Digges, Jeremiah (Josef Berger). Cape Cod Pilot. Provincetown, MA & New York, NY: Modern Pilgrim Press and Viking Press, 1937.

Doane, Doris. A Book of Cape Cod Houses. Old Greenwich, CT: The Chatham Press, Inc., 1972.

Doane, Doris. Exploring Old Cape Cod. Chatham, MA: The Chatham Press, Inc., 1968.

Eastham Tercentenary Committee. Eastham Massachusetts, 1651-1951. Eastham, MA: Eastham Tercentenary Committee, 1951.

Eaton, John P. and Charles A. Haas. Titanic – Destination Disaster. New York, NY: W. W. Norton, 1996.

Echeverria, Donald. A History of Billingsgate. Wellfleet, MA: Wellfleet Historical Society, 1991.

Fawsett, Marise. Cape Cod Annals. Bowie, MD: Heritage Books, Inc., 1990.

Farson, Robert. Cape Cod Railroads: Including Martha's Vineyard and Nantucket. Yarmouth Port, MA: Cape Cod Historical Publications, 1990.

Farson, Robert. The Cape Cod Canal. Middletown, CT: Wesleyan University Press, 1977.

Fisher, Charles E. The Story of the Old Colony Railroad. Fall River, MA: Frank P. Dubiel, 1974.

Freeman, Frederick. The History of Cape Cod. Yarmouth Port, MA: Parnassus Imprints, 1965.

Fritze, Hattie Blossom. Horse & Buggy Days on Old Cape Cod. Barnstable, MA: Great Marshes Press, 1966.

Frost, Jack. A Cape Cod Sketchbook. New York, NY: Coward-McCann, Inc, 1939.

Gamble, Adam. 1880 Atlas of Barnstable County. Yarmouthport, MA: On Cape Publications, 1998.

Giambarba, Paul. The Picture Story of Cape Cod. Centerville, MA: The Scrimshaw Press: 1965.

Gibson, Marjorie Hubbell. Historical & Genealogical Atlas and Guide to Barnstable County. Teaticket, MA: Falmouth Genealogical Society, 1995.

Green, Eugene and William Sachse. Names of the Land. Chester, CT: Globe Pequot Press, 1983.

Griffis, William Elliot. The Pilgrims in Their Three Homes. New York, NY: Houghton, Mifflin & Co., 1898.

Henderson, Eleanor. A Short History of Transportation in Chatham. Privately Printed.

Hill, Dewey D. & Elliott R. Hughes. Ice Harvesting in Early America. New Hartford, NY: New Hartford Historical Society, 1977.

Inquirer & Mirror. A Brief History of Nantucket's 300 Years. Nantucket, MA, 1959.

Ivanoff, Josephine Buck. Pieces of Old Cape Cod. Jack Claire Viall, 1985.

Jalbert, Russel R. Where Sea & History Meet - 4000 Years of Life in Orleans. Orleans, MA: Orleans Bicentennial Commission, 1997.

Johnson, Jack. Stories of Cape Cod. Plymouth, MA: Memorial Press of Plymouth, 1944.

Jones, Jr., Joseph C. America's Icemen. Humble, TX: Jobeco Books, 1984.

Kane, Tom. My Pamet. Mount Kisco, NY: Moyer Bell Limited, 1989.

Keene, Betsey D. History of Bourne from 1622 to 1937. Yarmouthport, MA: Charles W. Swift, 1937.

King, H. Roger. Cape Cod & Plymouth Colony in the Seventeenth Century. Lanham, MD: University Press of America, 1994.

Kinney, Charles P. A History of Dennis Union Church. Dennis, MA: Dennis Union Church, 1991.

Kittredge, Henry C. Cape Cod: It's People & Their History. Boston, MA: Houghton Mifflin Company, 1968.

Kittredge, Henry C. Mooncussers of Cape Cod. New York, NY: Houghton Mifflin Co., 1937.

Kittredge, Henry C. Shipmasters of Cape Cod. Boston, MA & New York, NY: Houghton Mifflin Company, 1935.

Knowles, Katharine. Cape Cod Journey. Barre, MA: Barre Publishers, 1966.

Lawson, Evelyn. Yesterday's Cape Cod. Miami, FL: E.A. Seemann Publishing, Inc., 1975.

Leighton, Clare. Where Land Meets Sea. Chatham, MA: The Chatham Press, Inc., 1973.

Lincoln, Joseph C. Cape Cod Yesterdays. New York, NY: Blue Ribbon Books, 1939.

Lombard Jr., Asa Cobb Paine. East of Cape Cod. New Bedford, MA: Reynolds-De Walt Printing, Inc, 1976.

Lord, Walter. A Night to Remember. New York, NY: Bantam Books, 1955.

Lovell, Jr., R.A. Sandwich – A Cape Cod Town. Sandwich, MA: Town of Sandwich Archives & Historical Center, 1984.

Lowe, Alice A. Nauset on Cape Cod - A History of Eastham. Eastham, MA: Eastham Historical Society, 1968.

Monbleau, Marcia J. The Cape Playhouse. South Yarmouth, MA: Allen D. Bragdon Publishers, Inc., 1991.

Monk, Lillian Hoag. Old Pilgrim Days. Los Angeles, CA: H. A. Miller Co., 1920.

Morris, Paul C. and Joseph F. Morin. The Island Steamers. Nantucket, MA: Nantucket Nautical Publishers, 1977.

Neal, Allan. Cape Cod is a Number of Things. Yarmouth Port, MA: The Register Press, 1954.

Noble, Frederick A. The Pilgrims. Cambridge, MA: The University Press, 1907.

O'Neil, Neva. Master Mariners of Dennis. Dennis, MA: Dennis Historical Society, 1965.

Otis, Amos. Genealogical Notes of Barnstable Families. Barnstable, MA: F.B. & F.P. Goss Publishers and Printers, 1888.

Quinn, William P. Shipwrecks Around Cape Cod. Orleans, MA: Lower Cape Publishing, 1973.

Quinn, William P. The Saltworks of Historic Cape Cod. Orleans, MA: Parnassus Imprint, 1993.

Reid, Nancy Thacher. Dennis, Cape Cod. Dennis, MA: Dennis Historical Society, 1996.

Reid, William James. The Building of the Cape Cod Canal. Privately Printed, 1961.

Reynard, Elizabeth. The Narrow Land. Chatham, MA: Chatham Historical Society, 1978.

Ryder, Marion Crowell. Cape Cod Remembrances. Taunton, MA: William S. Sullwold Publishing, 1972.

Schwind, Phil. Making a Living Alongshore. Camden, ME: International Marine Publishing Co, 1976.

Sheedy, Jack & Debi Boucher Stetson. The Insider's Guide to Cape Cod. Manteo, NC: Insider's Publishing, Inc., 1997.

Small, Isaac M. Shipwrecks on Cape Cod. Chatham, MA: The Chatham Press, Inc., 1967.

Smith, Mary Lou. The Book of Falmouth: A Tercentennial Celebration 1686-1986. Falmouth, MA: Falmouth Historical Society, 1986

Smith, Mary Lou. Woods Hole Reflections. Woods Hole, MA: Woods Hole Historical Society, 1983.

Snow, Edward Rowe. A Pilgrim Returns to Cape Cod. Boston, MA: The Yankee Publishing Co., 1946.

Snow, Edward Rowe. New England Sea Tragedies. New York, NY. Dodd, Mead & Co., 1960.

Snow, Edward Rowe. The Lighthouses of New England. New York, NY: Dodd, Mead & Co., 1945

Sokolosky, William C. A History of Railroads in Yarmouth, Mass. Yarmouthport, MA: Historical Society of Old Yarmouth, 1975.

Sprague, Mary A. A Cape Cod Village. Hyannis, MA: The Patriot Press, 1963.

Stetson, Judy. Wellfleet – A Pictorial History. Wellfleet, MA: The Wellfleet Historical Society, 1963.

Swift, Charles F. Cape Cod. Yarmouthport, MA: Register Publishing Company, 1897.

Swift, Charles F. History of Old Yarmouth. Yarmouthport, MA: The Historical Society of Old Yarmouth, 1975.

Tarbell, Arthur Wilson. Cape Cod Ahoy. Boston, MA: A.T. Ramsay and Co, 1932.

Thoreau, Henry David. Cape Cod. New York, NY: Bramhall House, 1951.

Town of Barnstable. The Seven Villages of Barnstable. Barnstable, MA: Town of Barnstable, 1976.

Trayser, Donald G. Barnstable: Three Centuries of a Cape Cod Town. Hyannis, MA: F.B. & F.P. Goss, 1939.

Various. About Cape Cod. Boston, MA: Thomas Todd Company, 1936.

Vuilleumier, Marion. Cape Cod - A Pictorial History. Norfolk, VA: The Donning Co., 1982.

Vuilleumier, Marion. Churches of Cape Cod. Taunton, MA: Wm. S. Sullwold Publishing, 1974.

Vuilleumier, Marion. Earning a Living on Olde Cape Cod. Craigville, MA: Craigville Press, 1968.

Vuilleumier, Marion. Indians on Olde Cape Cod. Taunton, MA: Wm. S. Sullwold Publishing, 1970.

Vuilleumier, Marion. Sketches of Old Cape Cod. Taunton, MA: Wm. S. Sullwold Publishing, 1972.

Vuilleumier, Marion. The Town of Yarmouth, Massachusetts - A History: 1639-1989. Yarmouth, MA: The Historical Society of Old Yarmouth, 1989.

Willison, George P. Saints & Strangers. New York, NY: Time, Inc. 1964.

Wood, Donald. Cape Cod - A Guide. Boston, MA: Little, Brown & Co., 1973.

Woods Hole, Martha's Vineyard & Nantucket Steamship Authority. Lifeline to the Islands. Woods Hole, MA, 1977.

Yarmouth Historical Commission. Yarmouth – Old Homes and Gathering Places. Yarmouth, MA, 1989.

ADDITIONAL NOTES

CHAPTER 1

A Sense of Where We Were
Cape Codder newspaper, Phil Schwind, March 25, 1965; Directory of Massachusetts Place Names, compiled by Charlotte Pease Davis for the Massachusetts Daughters of the American Revolution, Bay State News, Lexington, MA, 1987; Names of the Land, Eugene Green and William L. Sachse.

Necks
Cape Cod and Islands Atlas and Guide Book, Volume V, Butterworth Company of Cape Cod, Inc., West Yarmouth, MA, 1982; Cape And Islands Locater, John W. Davenport, First Impressions, Madison, Wisconsin, 1989; Cape Cod National Seashore Trails Illustrated Map, Trails Illustrated, a division of National Geographic Maps, Evergreen, Colorado, 1998.

A Place Called Punkhorn
Sand in Their Shoes: A Cape Cod Reader, Edith and Frank Shay, Houghton Mifflin Co., Boston, MA, 1951, pages 333 & 334.

Upper and Lower Cape Cod
Cape Cod and the Islands: The Geologic Story, Robert Oldale, Parnassus Imprints, East Orleans, MA, 1992, page 3; A Geologist's View of Cape Cod, American Museum of Natural History, the Natural History Press, Garden City, NY, 1966.

Physic Point
Physic Point: Memoirs of Hyannis, 1914-1929, Alvah W. Bearse, The Patriot Press, Hyannis, MA., 1982; History of Wellfleet: From the Early Days to Present Times, Everett I. Nye, 1920.

CHAPTER 2

Introduction
The Cape Codder, Geneva Eldredge, January 19, 1956; The Cape Codder, "Once Upon a Time on Cape Cod," Gustavus Swift Paine, December 15, 1955, page 5.

Moons Over Stage Harbor
Samuel de Champlain: Father of New France, Samuel Eliot, Morison, Little, Brown and Company, Boston, MA, 1972, page 83; Cape Cod: Its People and Their History, Henry C. Kittredge, Houghton Mifflin Company, Boston, MA, 1968, pages 16-18.

Mooncussers
Mooncussers of Cape Cod, Henry Kittredge; Days to Remember, Joshua Atkins Nickerson 2nd, Chatham Historical Society, Chatham, MA, 1988, page 204.

Trying to Forget the Alamo
The Falmouth Enterprise, May 25, 1962; A Time to Stand, Walter Lord, Bonanza Books, New York, N.Y., 1987 edition, pages 26 and 97-98.

The Harwich Killer
Cape Cod Times, "A Harwich Relic of Battle Represents a Deadly History," James J. Coogan Jr., November 27, 1983, page 17.

America's First Vietnam War Started by Cape Codder!
"Mad Jack": The Biography of Captain John Percival USN, 1789-1862, David F. Long, Greenwood Press, Westport, CT, 1993, Chapter 12; Yankee Magazine, Alton H. Blackington, July 1961, page 41.

The Wellfleet Oysterman
Cape Cod, Henry David Thoreau, Bramhall House Edition, W.W. Norton & Company, Inc., New York, NY, 1951, page 81.

CHAPTER 3

Introduction
Dennis, Cape Cod: From Firstcomers to Newcomers 1639-1993, Nancy Thacher Reid, Dennis Historical Society, Dennis, MA, 1996, pages 437-439; Yarmouth Register, March 22, 1940; Yarmouth Register, August 21, 1942.

The Importance of Being Otis
Yarmouth Register, compiled by Donald Trayser, June 11, 1948, page 7; The Otis Family in Provincial and Revolutionary Massachusetts, John J. Waters, Jr., University of North Carolina Press, Chapel

Hill, NC; 1968, pages 199-203.

Cinderella was a Cape Codder!
The gravestone of Cinderella Cole can be found in the South Wellfleet Cemetery off Route 6 just beyond the Wellfleet Theatre. She died on December 1, 1905 at age 78 years, 8 months, and 18 days. The stones for Snow and White represent the graves of George E. Snow (1870-1933) and Alice White (1905-1993) and are at the cemetery located west of the Dennis Union Church in Dennis village.

"A Bigger Set of Rascals"
Before the Wind: The Memoir of an American Sea Captain, 1808-1833, edited by Susan Fels, Penguin Books, New York, NY, 1999.

The Girl Who Was Named for a Shipwreck
The Descendants of Robert Linnell, by Rachel Linnell Wynn, Gateway Press, Inc., Baltimore, MD, 1994. page 33; The Barnstable Patriot, Vol., XXVII, no. 33., February 3, 1857, page 3; A History of Early Orleans, Ruth L. Barnard, Orleans Historical Society, Orleans, MA, 1975, page 97.

The Man Who Never Slept
Cape Cod Standard Times, January 4, 1939, pages 1 and 2; Yankee Magazine, "The Man Who Never Slept," Bill Schofield, January 1994, pages 74-77.

Frank Cabral's Wild Ride
Yankee Magazine, June 1969, page 88; Cape Cod Standard Times, June 28, 1948, page 1; Provincetown Advocate, July 1, 1948, page 1.

Harry's Ashes
Harry Kemp: The Last Bohemian, William Brevda, Bucknell University Press, London, England, 1986; Provincetown as a Stage, Leona Rust Egan, Parnassus Imprints, Orleans, MA., 1994, pages 251-255; Compass Grass Anthology: A Collection of Provincetown Portraits , Josephine Couch Del Deo, Three Dunes Press, Provincetown, MA, 1983, pages 1-5.

CHAPTER 4

Thumpertown
Names of the Land, Eugene Green and William Sachse; Cape Cod Life, "Hallelujah!: Spiritual Revival in the 1800's," Ruth Howard Foley, Summer, 1981; Eastham Massachusetts 1651-1951, Eastham Tercentenary Committee, Eastham, MA., 1951, pages 43-45; The Story of the Yarmouth Camp Ground and the Methodist Camp Meetings on Cape Cod, Irving Lovell, privately printed, 1985.

The Roller Skating Rink that Became a Church
Truro, Cape Cod, As I Knew It, Anthony L. Marshall, Vantage Press, Inc., New York, NY, 1974, pages 88-91.

The Church that Came in from the Sea
Yankee Magazine, "The Church that Came in on the Tide," Sumner A. Towne, Jr., June, 1967, page 81; Bourne Courier, "The Little Church That Came in With the Tide," Michael Burgess, March 26, 1992; Interview with Helen Farrell, the daughter of Reverend John Stevenson.

CHAPTER 5

The Fastest Clipper Captain
Greyhounds of the Sea: The Story of the American Clipper Ship, Carl C. Cutler, Halcyon House, New York, NY, 1930, pages 266-268; Shipmasters of Cape Cod, Henry C. Kittredge, Houghton Mifflin Co., Boston, MA, 1930, pages 167-169.

A Seafaring Cape Cod Town Without a Harbor
Shipmasters of Cape Cod, Henry C. Kittredge; Brewster Shipmasters, J. Henry Sears, The Register Press, Yarmouthport, MA, 1906.
Cape Cod Yesterdays, Joseph Lincoln and Harold Brett, Little, Brown and Co., Boston, MA, 1935, pages 38-45.

The Last Coasterman
"Captain Bennett Dottridge Coleman," Historical Society of Santuit and Cotuit, based on lecture by Mrs. Allan Freeman Robbins on July 11, 1969; The Last Sail Down East, Giles M.S. Tod; Interview with Mr. and Mrs. Allan Robbins of Teaticket, relatives of Captain Coleman; Barnstable Patriot, Thursday June 9, 1927, page 3

CHAPTER 6

Lost at Sea!
Epitaphs and Icons: A Guide to the Burying Grounds of Cape Cod, Martha's Vineyard and Nantucket, Diana Hume George and Malcolm A. Nelson.

When Family Ties Kept a Lighthouse Bright
Interview with Bruce Garfield, a descendant of Captain William Garfield of West Dennis.

Women of the Lights
Lighthouses of Cape Cod, Martha's Vineyard, and Nantucket: Their History and Lore, Admont G. Clark, Parnassus Imprints, East Orleans, MA, 1992, pages 33, 34, 80, and 95; Women Who Kept the Lights: An Illustrated History of Female Lighthouse Keepers, Mary Louise Clifford and J. Candace Clifford, Cypress Communications, Williamsburg, VA, 1993, pages 106 and 160; History of Barnstable County, Simeon L. Deyo, 1890, pages 556 and 793.

The Strange Loss of the Carrie D. Knowles
Provincetown Advocate, May 6, 1909, page 2; Provincetown Advocate, May 13, 1909, page 2; Pamphlet written in 1979 and privately published by Georgia Knowles Ferguson, the granddaughter of the owner of the vessel; Interview with Carrie Knowles Cook, her mother and the namesake of the ship when she was over 100 years old and living in Hyannis.

The Shipwreck that Became a Clubhouse
Shipwrecks on Cape Cod, Isaac's M. Small, Chatham Press & Viking Press, Inc., 1970, pages 69-71.

CHAPTER 7

Not Just Another Smith
New England Galaxy, "Stephen Smith and His Rolltop Desk," Betty Bearse, Fall, 1972, pages 58-63.

The Man Who Challenged Cunard
The Great Liners, Melvin Maddocks, editor George G. Daniels, Volume 4 in a 21 volume series entitled "The Seafarers," Time Life Books, Alexandria, VA, 1978, pages 27-32; Queens of the Western Ocean: The Story of America's Mail and Passenger Sailing Lines, Carl C. Cutler, United States Naval Institute, Annapolis, MD, 1961; The American Heritage History of Seafaring America, Alexander Laing, editor Joseph J. Thorndike, American Heritage Publishing Co., New York, NY, 1974, pages 306 and 307; Shipmasters of Cape Cod, Henry C. Kittredge, Houghton Mifflin Co., Boston, MA, 1935, pages 127-135.

Caleb Chase – Cape Cod's "Coffee Baron"
The History of Barnstable County Massachusetts, Simeon L. Deyo, H.W. Blake & Co., New York, N.Y. 1890, page 869; The Yarmouth Register, December 19, 1908; Cape Codder, November 20, 1992, page 6; Cape Cod Chronicle, December 24, 1992; Boston Globe, January 3, 1993.

The South Yarmouth Wire Factory
The Town of Yarmouth, Massachusetts: A History 1639-1989, Marion Vuilleumier, Historical Society of Old Yarmouth, Yarmouthport, MA, 1989, pages 56, 97, and 127; The Cape, 1966, 1967.

The Captain and the Baby Carriage
History of Barnstable County, Simeon L. Deyo, 1890, page 873; Patent records were obtained from the Boston Public Library.

Skunks!
The Town of Yarmouth, Massachusetts: A History, 1639-1989, Marion Vuilleumier, Historical Society of Old Yarmouth, Yarmouthport, MA, 1989, page 98; Growing Up On Cape Cod, Donald B. Sparrow, Great Oaks Publishing Co., Eastham, MA, 1999, pages 141-144.

The Ambergris King
The Log of Provincetown and Truro on Cape Cod Massachusetts, Mellen C.M. Hatch, published privately in Provincetown, MA, 1939, page 76; There Goes Flukes, William Henry Tripp, Reynolds Printing, New Bedford, MA, 1938, chapter 7, pages 67-83; Cape Cod Magazine, Robert H. Cahoon, June 1916, pages 27 and 28; New York Herald, April 16, 1911, page 10.

Falmouth – America's Mushroom Capital
Cape Cod and All the Pilgrim Land, Lemuel C. Hall, August, 1921, page 15; The History of Falmouth, article by Harry C. Richardson's, edited by Mary Lou Smith, pages 70-72.

CHAPTER 8

A "No" Vote on Independency!
History of Cape Cod. Frederick Freeman, Volume II pages 309-313; Cape Cod: Its People and Their History, Henry C. Kittredge, pages 126 and 127.

Enoch Crosby – Revolutionary Spy
Oddity Odyssey: A Journey Through New England's Colorful Past, James Chenoweth, Henry Holt and Company, New York, NY, 1996, pages 88, 89; Vital Records of the Town of Harwich, Massachusetts, Harwich Historical Society, 1982, page 69; History of Barnstable County, Simeon L. Deyo, page 254; New England Magazine, "The Spy of the Neutral Ground," Harry Edward Miller, Volume 18, pages 307-319.

The Ransom of the Saltworks
The History of Cape Cod: Annals of the Thirteen Towns of Barnstable County, Frederick Freeman, W.H. Piper and Co., 1862, Volume II page 754; Cape Cod: Its People and Their History, Henry Kittredge, Houghton Mifflin Company, Boston, MA, 1968, pages 134-144; Cape Cod Standard Times, "Brewster Kowtowed in 1814," May 12, 1972, page 17; The Register, Spring 1973, Byways Supplement with an article by Charles Holbrook; The Saltworks of Historic Cape Cod, William P. Quinn, Parnassus Imprints, Orleans, Ma. 1993; Brewster Historical Society, original letter of Commander Ragget to the town of Brewster.

Slavery and Cape Cod
Cape Cod: Its People and Their History, Henry C. Kittredge, Houghton Mifflin Company, Boston, MA, 1968, pages 63-67; Paines's History of Harwich references Mrs. Samuel Hall selling three slaves in 1756 to her nephew John Allen; Charles Swift's History of Old Yarmouth cites Benjamin Homer of Yarmouth purchasing a slave on February 20, 1776; Agnes Edwards' Cape Cod Old and New, page 43; The quote from the Sandwich town meeting can be found in Freeman's History of Cape Cod, pages 114, 115; The story of Hector the last slave in Truro is found in Shebnah Rich's Truro-Cape Cod, pages 226-229; Reference to George Thomas Washington can be found in an article by James Quirk in the Cape Cod Times, July 4, 1976, page 18; Cape Codder, Susanna Graham-Pye, June 23, 1998, pages 3-5.

The Man with the Branded Hand
Provincetown Advocate, September 3, 1877; Provincetown Advocate, March 14, 1878, page 4; The Branded Hand: Trial and Imprisonment of Johnathan Walker at Pensacola, Florida, 1845, Bicentennial Project of the State of Florida, 1976; Cape Codder, "Branded Hand Made Harwich's Walker a Martyr for Abolition," Carol Snowdon, March 22, 1988; "The Man With the Branded Hand," Mabel Weeks' 1902 prize essay for Harwich High School, Sturgis Library, Barnstable, Lothrop Collection under R. 929.2 Walker.

Cape Cod's Civil War General
Generals in Blue: Lives of the Union Commanders, Ezra J. Warner, Louisiana State Press, 1964; Cape Cod Standard Times, "Gen. Joe: Cape's Brightest in Civil War," George Moses, January 12, 1975, editorial page; History of Old Yarmouth, Charles Swift, edited by Charles A. Holbrook, Jr., Historical Society of Old Yarmouth, Yarmouthport, MA, 1975, pages 222 and 223; The Historical Society of Old Yarmouth, Captain Bangs Hallet House, Yarmouthport, MA.

The Mutual Support Club
Truro Cape Cod, or Land Marks and Sea Marks, Shebnah Rich, D. Lothrop and Company, Boston, MA, page 474.

Fort "Useless"
Cape Cod Times, December 12, 1980.

CHAPTER 9

Brewster and the Lost Dauphin
The Primal Place, by Robert Finch. Published by W.W. Norton, New York, N.Y., 1983, pages 107-137.

A Trip on the River Queen
History of Barnstable County, Simeon L. Deyo, page 971; Cape Cod Standard Times, George L. Moses, April 25, 1971; The Story of the Island Steamers, Harry B Turner, Inquirer and Mirror Press, Nantucket, MA, 1910, pages 66-68.

Helen Keller and Brewster
"Some Brewster Beginnings," Brewster Historical Society, Founder's Day, February 19, 1979; The Saints of Brewster 1856-1996, Paul Saint, privately published, 1996, page 34.

Grover Cleveland's Cape Cod Secret
American Heritage Magazine, "When the President Disappeared," John Stuart Martin, October 1957, pages 10-13 and 102-103; New York Times, July 4, 1893; New York Times, July 5, 1893; New York Times, July 6, 1893.

"Tiger of Vendee" at Yarmouth
Yesterday's Tide, Florence W. Baker, privately printed, 1941, pages 223-229.

Prisoners of War
Falmouth Enterprise, "War Prisoners' Life in Edward's Stockade," July 14, 1944; Falmouth Enterprise, "Germans Salvage Hurricane Timber," May 18, 1945; Collected research of Dr. Robert F. Phelan ,William Brewster Nickerson Room, Cape Cod Community College, Barnstable, MA.

The Song that Made Cape Cod Famous
Cape Cod Times, August 21, 1997, page 1; "Old Cape Cod" was copyrighted in 1956 by George Pincus and Sons Music Corporation, New York, NY.

The New Pilgrims
Cape Cod Standard Times, July 21, 1948, page 1; Cape Cod Standard Times, July 22, 1948, page 1; Provincetown Advocate, July 22, 1948, pages 1 and 7.

CHAPTER 10

Introduction
Cape Cod Architecture, Claire Baisley, Parnassus Imprints, Inc., Orleans, MA, 1989, pages 185 and 186; The Register, "Mobile Homes," by Ted Frothingham, November 14, 1974, section II, page 1; Cape Cod Life, "Finding New Homes for Old Houses: A Moving Experience," by Christie Lowrance, Issue #2, Early Summer, 1983, pages 46-51; Provincetown Advocate, October 23, 1969.

Cape's Oldest Mill is Not on Cape Cod!
Cape Cod Magazine, January 15, 1928; The Town of Yarmouth, Massachusetts: A History, 1639-1989, Marion Vuilleumier, Historical Society of Old Yarmouth, 1989, pages 119, 145,146.

Cape Cod Skyscraper
The Birth of a Building: The Harwich Exchange, Virginia S. Doane, Jack Viall Press, West Harwich, MA, 1965; At Home: Harwich Cape Cod Massachusetts, Marcia J. Monbleau, privately printed, 1993, pages 166-169; The Harwich Historical Society, Brooks Academy Historical Center, Harwich, MA.

CHAPTER 11

First in Flight?
Cape Cod Magazine, "When Flying Was Mostly Falling," May 1926, page 10.

Speed Trap!
The Barnstable Patriot, July 17, 1905, page 2; The Barnstable Patriot, July 31, 1905, page 2; The Register, "Cape Cod: Home of the first speed trap," Evan J. Albright, July 22, 1999, page 12.

The First Traffic Rotary
The Town of Yarmouth, Massachusetts: A History, 1639-1989, Marion Vuilleumier, Historical Society of Old Yarmouth, 1989; Cape Cod Times, Julia St. George, February 13, 1995, page A7; Cape Cod Magazine, September 1916, pages 5-7; Boston Globe, "A Concept Comes Full Circle," Beth Carney, October 3, 1999, section 3, page 8.

Blame it on Hoover
The Seven Villages of Barnstable, Vail-Ballou Press/Town of Barnstable, New York, NY, 1976; The Register, "West Barnstable Brick Empire Leaves Legacy of Memories and $22 Bricks," Martha Cusick, Section II, April 27, 1978, pages 1 and 2; The Village Advertiser, C. I. Mahoney, March 17, 1983, page 8; Cape Cod Life, "30 Million Bricks a Year! That was the West Barnstable Brick Company," Henry Scammell, Spring 1984; Whelden Library, West Barnstable Village.

Spring in Hyannis ... All Year Long
While there is no written history of the telephone company on Cape Cod, a fair number of the village switchboard operators are still alive and to this day retain, and occasionally dispense, much of the overheard gossip of an earlier age.

The authors wish to recognize the contributions of all the libraries, museums, historical societies, and archives across the Cape that provided much valuable information toward the research and writing of this book.

ABOUT THE AUTHORS

Jim Coogan was raised on Cape Cod and grew up in Brewster. Retired from almost three decades in the classroom as a high school history teacher, he is now able to pursue his special interest of Cape Cod history. Jim is a popular lecturer and writer about Cape Cod and is currently a regular columnist for the *Cape Cod Times*. In 1985 he wrote a chapter for the book *Three Centuries of a Cape Cod County: Barnstable, Massachusetts, 1685-1985*. In 1999, he co-authored *Cape Cod Companion*, with Jack Sheedy and he is a frequent contributor to area magazines and newspapers. He lives in Dennis with his wife Beth and their affectionate and very headstrong Great Dane puppy, Sussannah.

Jack Sheedy has been freelancing for *The Barnstable Patriot* since 1985 and has been a contributor to, and managing editor of, the award-winning history magazine *Summerscape* for a number of years. He also writes for other publications, including *Cape Cod Guide Magazine*, and has written for the John F. Kennedy Library. He has published nearly 300 articles and has authored four other books, including *Dennis Journal, The Insider's Guide to Cape Cod, Nantucket & Martha's Vineyard*, and *Cape Cod Companion* (written with Jim Coogan). Jack lives in East Dennis with his wife Adriana, their children Gregory and Melissa, and their Boston Terrier, Lucy.

ABOUT THE BARNSTABLE PATRIOT

The Barnstable Patriot, founded in 1830, is published weekly in Hyannis and remains the third oldest continuously operating newspaper in New England. It charts the activities, large and less so, of the town of Barnstable's seven villages and records the events which comprise the town's life, both public and private. *The Patriot* engages the issues of the day in town and on Cape fully cognizant of the past and fiercely hopeful of the future. Samples of *The Patriot's* weekly fare can be found at their web site **www.barnstablepatriot.com**.

ABOUT CAPE COD GUIDE MAGAZINE

Cape Cod Guide Magazine is published six times a year, detailing the many events and attractions throughout the Cape's fifteen towns and of interest to the peninsula's tourists and year round residents alike. The magazine also features articles focusing on the Cape's rich history, as well as town tours, places to visit, and is accented with many fine photos of the area's landmarks. *Cape Cod Guide Magazine* can be found at many stores and establishments around the Cape. The magazine's web site is **www.capecodguide.com**.

ACKNOWLEDGMENTS

First and foremost, I would like to thank my wife Beth for her support and good humor, as I continued to use time spent in writing this book as an excuse to avoid cleaning out the garage. There is very little that I ever write that doesn't get subjected to her levelheaded scrutiny before it goes to publication. Mary Sicchio, the current archivist in the William Brewster Nickerson Room of Cape Cod materials at Cape Cod Community College was, once again, a prime source of assistance and support. I should also like to express my gratitude and appreciation to Charlotte Price, a former archivist in the Nickerson Room, who provided me with lots of material for some of the stories in this book. When it seemed that I couldn't think of something to write about, Charlotte would always strategically place several packets of documents, publications, or sources in front of me and encourage me to "just get started." So many people gave me unusual stories to follow up and interesting directions to travel. Bruce Garfield, Bonnie Snow, Helen Farrell, Bob Coleman, John Sears, Beverly Thacher, and Georgia Ferguson have their own places in this book because they set me on a trail to solve some puzzle of Cape Cod history. There are many others that made similar contributions, including some of my students and faculty colleagues at Dennis-Yarmouth Regional High School. Finally, I owe a great debt of thanks to Jack Sheedy, my co-writer who has made me believe that I am just as much a writer as I am an historian.

John Cooge

Any message of acknowledgement would have to begin with a heartfelt "thank you" to my wife, Adriana. She has endured many years of my mind wandering away from the subject at hand in favor of some piece of Cape Cod history or some article I was in the midst of writing. She often critiques my work, providing useful advice and unwavering support. I also would like to thank her for the contributions she made to this particular book, by proofreading the text and by taking a number of the photographs that appear within it, as well as the photo of Jim and myself that appears on the back cover. I wish to also thank my children, Melissa and Gregory, who in many cases tag along with me to historical sites and libraries, perhaps in hopes that I will remember them with an ice cream cone or a cup of clam chowder on the way home. Thanks to Rob and Toni Sennott, publishers of *The Barnstable Patriot*, as well as David Still II, the newspaper's editor, for their constant support and guidance. Thanks also to Mike and Liz Rabideau, publishers and editors of *Cape Cod Guide Magazine*, for allowing me to contribute to their wonderful publication, and include some of those stories in this book. A huge amount of thanks goes to Kristen vonHentschel who contributed her graphic talents to the design of this book, from cover to cover. I wish to recognize those who work at many of the libraries across the Cape, particularly in Dennis, Brewster, Yarmouth, Barnstable, and at Cape Cod Community College. Many a volume of ancient history or forgotten lore was entrusted to me, and for that I would like to express my appreciation. Lastly, I offer my deepest gratitude to my co-author, Jim Coogan. He has become more than a co-author, but a good and trusted friend who shares my interest in history and in keeping the old stories of Cape Cod alive for future generations.

Jack Sheedy

The front cover image, from Jim Coogan's collection, is entitled "Old Fisherman" from an early twentieth century postcard printed by The Leighton & Valentine Co., New York, NY. The back cover photograph is by Adriana Sheedy. All postcards in this book are from Jim Coogan's collection. Chapter 6: "U.S. Wireless Station and Highland Light, North Truro, Cape Cod, Mass." printed by Curt Teich & Co., Inc., Chicago, IL and distributed by E.D. West Co., South Yarmouth, MA. Chapter 9: "Gray Gables, Buzzards Bay, Mass." printed by This is Holmes, Brockton and Onset Bay, MA. Chapter 10: "The Oldest Windmill on Cape Cod"printed by H.A. Dickerman & Son, Taunton, MA; "Swedenborgian Church, Yarmouthport, Mass." printed by Souvenir Post Card Co., New York, NY. Chapter 11: "State Highway, Cape Cod, Mass." printed by H.A. Dickerman & Son, Taunton, Mass.